To Janeen

BEHIND THESE 4 WALLS

Thank you for your support
I pray this book is A
BLESSING to you!!
Pay It forward!!!

EBONI STEWART

Love & BLESSINGS

EB

Published and distributed in the United States by Eboni Stewart, Rosedale, New York

Copyright © 2020 by Eboni Stewart
All rights reserved. No parts of this book may be reproduced by any mechanical, photographic, or electronic process, or in the form of phonographic recording. This book may not be stored in a retrieval system, transmitted, or otherwise be copied for public or private use – other than for "fair use" as brief quotations embodied in articles and reviews – without prior written permission of the publisher.

The author of this book does not dispense medical advice or prescribe any technique as a form of treatment for physical or emotional problems. The author intends to offer information of a general nature to help you in your quest for emotional and spiritual well-being. In the event you use any of the information in this book for yourself, which is your constitutional right, the author or publisher assume no responsibility for your actions.

Scriptures found at www.biblegateway.com

Book Coach – The Self-Publishing Maven
Cover Design – Okomota
Editing – Robin Devonish and Deborah Perspective, LLC.
Interior Design – Istvan Szabo, Ifj., Sapphire Guardian International
Photography – Tyquane "PhotosByKai" Bates
Proofreading – Deborah Perspective, LLC

ISBN 13: 978-1-7352780-0-1

Printed in the United States of America

ACKNOWLEDGEMENTS

To my parents Bishop James B. Jones III, and Pastor Joyce A. Jones, thank you for all you've instilled in me. Mom, thank you for having me! You have given me the firm foundation I needed to become the woman I am today. Thank you for giving me JESUS at a young age. You've taught me how to be strong in the Lord, and your strength is relentless. YOU ARE MY SHERO! I am eternally grateful for the love and sacrifices you've made.

To my parents in love, Mr. and Mrs. John A. Stewart, thank you! Ma Edna, I appreciate your support, and birthing my *'soul mate.'* I am eternally grateful!

My prayer for you all is that your latter years will be *greater,* and you all will continue to enjoy the fruit of your labor.

To our Spiritual Parents, Apostle Mike, and Dr. Dee Dee Freeman, words cannot express the gratitude that I have for you both! Through your ministry, spiritual guidance, and leadership, I have grown by leaps and bounds. We are experiencing Kingdom Living on earth because of you! The vision of godly examples you both provide for my family, and I are simply *priceless.* Only God can repay you both for what you've sown into us. We love you for all you do, not to mention your Swag and Anointing! It's an honor to serve *true generals* in the body of Christ.

Apostle, thank you for being you! You are the epitome of what a *spiritual father* should be, John and I are *grateful*. Dr. Dee, thank you for being there during some of my darkest moments. Your talks, revelation, instructions, and encouraging words have been healing to my soul.

To my siblings Jayvon, Jamise, and James IV, whom I love dearly! My brother in love "Uncle Pee" and my main man Mr. Pierre "JoJo" Porterfield Jr., my sister in love, Taneka Jones, and all my beautiful nieces and nephew. Thank you for being you! You all have a special place in my heart. Thank you for your love and support.

To my "Secret Reader" Tanjanika A. Clark, big sister, and cousin, thank you for being the big sister! Thank you for telling me, "Eb, this is good!" You read each chapter for me and encouraged me to keep writing! You'll never know how much *I Love You*.

To my aunts, cousins, and family near and far, you are all very special to me! Thank you for all you have contributed to my life.

To my Mentoring for Success Family! The beautiful thing about God is when you set yourself to minister to others, He also ministers to you! Through our bond of loving, supporting, and empowering one another, I have indeed grown and matured in Christ. Thank you for allowing me to serve you, and I pray that your lives have been made better through our journey of self-work. Always remember to pay it forward! Self-Work is better when we do it TOGETHER!

To all our friends, loved ones, and mentees, you all know who you are. I appreciate you all, Love You To Life!

Last but never least to The Self-Publishing Maven, Robin E. Devonish! Thank you for all the hard work you put into this book. Thank you for reading and re-reading, editing, tweaking, and publishing this book. You took care of my project like it was your own. Thank you for your honesty, support, and commitment. Most of all, thank you for your encouraging words and for believing in the author in me. I pray a Bible promise return to you for all that you have done for me. Many Blessings!

DEDICATION

I dedicate this book to the woman who started it all, my grandmother Esther Eunice Muldrow. She was a true example of the Proverbs 31 woman. She would always hug me, pat me on my butt and say, "There is something special about you." I'm grateful that today I can wholeheartedly say, *I Believe Her.*

In loving memory of my Father Hylton Leroy Crayton, *Your Legacy Lives On*!

In loving memory of my cousin Naire' Lee McCormick, she was thriving, striving, and full of *Life*. Naire was on an amazing journey of self-work. I am proud to continue her legacy, she inspires me, and I will never stop working on bettering myself.

To my three most precious jewels, Jadé, Jaelyn, and Janiya, whom I have the honor and privilege to birth, "Mother" is one of the greatest titles in the world. You all are awesome, never cease to amaze me, and I am so grateful to be part of your lives. Watching you all grow and plant your feet into the 'Heart of Success' is returning the favor to me in so many ways, but most of all, *Thank You for Believing In Me!* You girls are my biggest cheerleaders and have given me the strength to push past my fears to believe that I can do all things through Christ. Thank you will never be enough. I pray your mommy has made you proud. I Love you "Stewart Girls" to LIFE! #FANTASTIC5

Last but certainly not least, *My King* and *My Babee* John Stewart, thank you for choosing me! I am honored to be called Mrs. Stewart!

Marrying you was the second-best decision to me giving my life to Christ. Thank you for being my soul mate, #1 encourager, supporter, confidant, mentor, and accountability partner. It's because of you that I endeavored on this journey of writing my first book. *You Always See and Bring Out The Best In Me!* I am eternally grateful to God for gifting me with you. Thank you for loving me like Christ loves the church. The Agape love we share gives us the ability to walk in our purpose. I pray everything you pour into me will be multiplied back to you through me, and then others. Forever your "Pumpkin."

CONTENTS

Introduction 1

Chapter I – Behind the 4 Walls of the Heart 5

Wall #1 – Hurt 5

Wall #2 – Forgiveness 12

Wall #3 – Knowing Who You Are 17

Wall #4 – Purpose 21

Chapter II – The 4 Walls of the Family 26

Wall #1 – Communication 26

Wall #2 – Transparency 32

Wall #3 – Accountability 37

Wall #4 – Unity 40

Chapter III – The 4 Walls of The Soul 44

Wall #1 – Salvation 50

Wall #2 – Renewing Your Mind 53

Wall #3 – A Progressive Lifestyle 57

Wall #4 – Sacrifice To Serve 62

Chapter IV – Behind The 4 Walls of Life 68

Wall #1 – Living a Learning Life 68

Wall #2 – Living a Life of Influence 74

Wall #3 – Living a Fruitful Life 79

Wall #4 – Living a Life of Expectation 87

Conclusion 94

Affirmations 95

INTRODUCTION

Have you ever felt like everyone around you appeared to be growing, maturing, and progressing in life? However, you've felt like you are just existing and stagnant. You are not alone. I can relate because I once felt that way too. The key to moving forward is to identify where you are and seek to work through those moments. Though you may be uncomfortable, that space is the perfect position to start working on your inner self.

When going through my moment, I realized that I felt stagnant because I was inconsistent with investing time or putting in the commitment and effort of building, transforming, and renewing my inner self.

After many years of committing to personal self-work, I took the information, knowledge, and principles I applied to my life and shared them with others. My sharing allowed me to become what I would like to call a "Spiritual Midwife." My heart desires to support, empower, and encourage others who commit to and go through the process of doing their *self-work* to become the best version of themselves.

When dealing with matters of the heart, family, our souls, and life, there is a lot to learn and work out. We must learn how to navigate in all those spaces, keeping in mind that we are a work in progress. The goal is to become healed, whole, and the person God wants you to be.

Behind These 4 Walls contains principles I've learned and the experiences I endured while working to be my best self. I believe the contents of this book will help you, if needed, get started on your journey of self-work to know who you are, whose you are, and understanding that you are here for a purpose. While reading, I want you to be encouraged, inspired, strengthened, and challenged in your thinking. My ultimate prayer is this book will spark the "why" in you and help your spirit and soul become one. The "why" I am speaking is not the motivational why. It's deeper than that. The question is 'why' do we not forgive, 'why' do we not change our habits, 'why' do we stay stagnant in the same place or 'why' do we hide behind so many walls? No matter what you go through, you must never stop working on *Yourself*.

Enjoy!
Love EB

> "Self-Work is BETTER
> when we do it TOGETHER!"

CHAPTER I –
BEHIND THE 4 WALLS OF THE HEART

During my husband and my journey of mentoring and supporting people through their most vulnerable times, coupled with our personal experience, and doing self-work, we noticed that many people struggle in the same areas. Our struggle may be in different ways or circumstances, but the core is in four, and the same, basic areas. I've concluded the four areas are usually Hurt, Forgiveness, Knowing Who We Are, and Purpose. At some point, we all will come face to face with each area.

When those four areas are not properly handled, they will become walls of defense, causing bitterness, anger, depression, low self-esteem, and a possible emotional shutdown. These four walls eventually stop us from growing and becoming all that God has created us to be.

John and I have many discussions about the heart and the walls associated with it. The information you are about to read is what we discovered and what blocks us from being 'Free To Be!'

WALL #1 – HURT

When talking about hurt, I usually begin by saying it's a universal language. No matter what kind of hurt you have experienced, you understand how it feels. The pain of rejection, mental or physical abuse from a friend, family, or a co-worker, no one can deny that hurt is unforgettable. Some people say that there are different levels of hurt. I am not here to debate that, but I do know when you are the person hurting, the pain feels like the worse kind to 'You.'

Simply put, hurt is universal, and we all can identify what it feels like to be emotionally, physically, or mentally hurt. We should show empathy to one another. The 'Great' news is that we 'All' can be 'Healed' from our hurt, no matter what kind of experience. 'God Promised' He would heal us from every 'Dis-ease.'

> "Bless and affectionately praise the LORD, O my soul, And do not forget any of His benefits; Who forgives all your sins, Who heals all your diseases; Who redeems your life from the pit, Who crowns you [lavishly] with lovingkindness and tender mercy; Who satisfies your years with good things, So that your youth is renewed like the [soaring] eagle. The LORD executes righteousness And justice for all the oppressed."
> — Psalms 103:2-6 AMP

When hurt, the first thing to do is confront the feeling and search ourselves. Take some quiet time to pray, meditate, and communicate with God; ask Him to reveal those areas of hurt. Sometimes we think we know why we are hurting, but it's necessary to inquire of Holy Spirit to reveal. You may be surprised by the revelation you receive.

During my journey of doing self-work, Holy Spirit revealed that much of my hurt was from childhood issues that were never dealt with. There is such a thing I call "Childhood Hurts." Many are still walking around upset about things they experienced as a child. This observation doesn't mean that one's entire childhood experience was horrible. Unfortunately, we are more affected by the few negative experiences encountered than the many positive ones. The key is to learn how to turn every negative experience into a positive one. When you pursue the action of positivity, you are no longer held back by the negative; the positive has pushed you 'forward!'

So, as I began to ask God specifically to define what kind of hurt affected me the most, He revealed *'abandonment'* was at the core of it. Did you know that 'hurt' has relatives? Sure does! And, although abandonment was my main issue, I found myself succumbing to its relatives, anger, negativity, rejection, low self-esteem, bitterness, and entitlement, to name a few.

Long story short, my biological father was not present in my life until around the age of 27. I would see him periodically, but due to his addictions, he was unable to be a supportive father.

I remember the first time I completely understood that my father had a problem. Although I did not have a close relationship with him, I often visited my paternal grandparents and aunt. I recall being at their house one evening when he came to the door, begging to use the bathroom and asking for food. You could tell that he was under the influence of something because he spoke loudly, was demanding, and aggressive. After a few moments of debate, he was allowed to come in. When he entered, there was a stench on him that was almost nauseating; as I write this, I can smell it now. Who would think that the fragrance was something I longed to smell on many days? It sounds a bit crazy, but it's true.

As I saw him walk through the house, I remember saying to myself, 'Wow, that man looks really bad.' Just as my grandparents promised, they allowed him to use the bathroom and gave him a wrapped-up plate of food to go. As he was walking down the stairs to exit, a relative turned to me and said, "You know that's your father, right?" I was younger than ten years old at the time. That day, it hit me. My father wasn't like the other dads I saw at school and around my neighborhood at the park or grocery store. I remember thinking to myself, "My father looks and acts like the homeless people I see living on the street." I believe that was the beginning of confusion for me, and unbeknownst to my mother, I was exposed to a lot of information that I couldn't begin to process as a child. Though he was unable to be there for me, I am forever grateful for my mother, who stepped in and played both roles. She is my SHERO. Her strength is powerful and amazing; she is the reason for the type of woman I am today.

My mom married when I was seven years old but by age 10, I consistently felt the emotional pain of wanting to know why my biological father was not present. Like most kids, I didn't know how to communicate these feelings, so I resorted to coming up with my own answers to the many questions in my mind. I would tell myself if I was prettier or had darker skin (both of my parents have darker skin than I) if I had longer hair, was smarter, more talented, or even if I were born a boy, he would have stayed. I eventually grew into feeling insecure about every part of who I was. I felt like I wasn't good enough physically, emotionally, or mentally. I learned how to perfect 'Self Negative Thinking' at a young age. I lacked an understanding of how the man who helped create me, the first man I ever loved could look at me and decide he didn't want to be a part of my life. I had mind meetings with myself and adjourned with all the wrong answers.

I became an incredibly angry teenager, but no one could tell. For the most part, I stayed quiet and just smiled. It's funny how the thing you focus on becomes the only thing you see. The abandonment was magnified, and every day all I could focus on was that my father didn't love me enough to stay.

'Eboni' Wisdom
This is why the Bible tells us in Psalms 34:3 to MAGNIFY the Lord. That means to make Him your focus, and eventually even in your daily routine He will be your only focus and His will will become the goal for every day.

As I continued to focus on missing him, the hurt became overwhelming. I began to fill the void by dating at the age of 14, making things more complicated. I found myself looking to boys my age to fill the void of me not having my father in my life. I was vulnerable, and the first boy who told me he loved me, became the guy that I gave my virginity to at 15. I was broken, empty, and gullible, searching for a type of "man's love." He made me feel protected, confident, secure, and worthy of love. He was everything I missed from my father. His attention validated who I was.

'Eboni' Wisdom
Little girls 'Desperately Need' their fathers or
a positive male role model in their lives.

This holds true if you are a young lady or raising one. What is also true is it takes a village! If the fathers or the village are absent, girls can or will begin to search for male companionship out of desperation.

I called myself dating this young man only to find he was a liar, even about me being his only girl. He was four years older and was in a long-term relationship with a young lady his age. I was devastated! Abandonment reared its ugly head again.

Thank God when I met my husband at age 15, we became great friends first. He was just one of the guys I could hang out with, talk to, and laugh with. The more we got to know each other, the more we realized we had much in common. Although his father was in the home, he could relate to my abandonment issues. John was very easy to talk to, and I felt very comfortable confiding in him. He always helped me to see the brighter side in every situation. With John, there was no pressure to be physical; we genuinely enjoyed each other's company. He became the person that I could be brutally honest with, without being judged. He treated me with respect, even after being exposed to my flaws. He encouraged the positivity in me and stimulated hope. With him, I could see a brighter future.

A few years later, we were seriously dating, and are together now 25 years and married for 20. But, just like many of us, when we don't deal with our childhood hurts, we carry them with us like a backpack throughout our lives. I was no different.

Early in my marriage, the anger, rage, and insecurities I had as a child began to magnify. I became more overwhelmed with those negative emotions and began to act out. I was a ticking time bomb, and any little thing would make me 'Go Off!' Not in a violent way, but I learned how to use my mouth like a knife and cut anyone who I felt was "coming for me." I was never a fighter, but if you took it there, the "Red Hook Brooklyn" would come out of me *'Quick!'* I lived the old saying, "I don't start fights, but I don't run from them either!" For the most part, my aggression was verbal, and I learned how to master being "Nice Nasty."

Reflective Moment
I am so 'Grateful' for my husband who understood
my pain and loved me through my hurt.

John was never abusive to me, nor did he react to my tantrums. He could have returned the favor several times. However, John responded by talking, working with me, and giving me the affection, support, and love I needed to overcome my hurt. Grateful is an understatement!

The Beginning of Healing

At the age of 27, I was reunited with my dad. He was clean and sober! I thought our reuniting would be one of the happiest days of my life. Instead, I was angry and overwhelmed with more negative emotions. It was then I realized that I had allowed the spirit of abandonment to overtake me. I not only felt abandoned by my father, I grew to feel rejected by everyone. I created a wall of anger in myself from ever feeling that pain again. Before I kn⌐ ment's relatives began visiting me. Loneliness, bitterness, low ⌐ esteem, and entitlement came over. I welcomed them in with open arms. In fact, I let them '*Move In*!' I felt so alone. The pain became too much for me. I couldn't handle it anymore. I appreciate my mom, who at a young age, taught me to call on Jesus when in trouble, feeling fearful, or in distress, and *He would Help Me*.

The memory of that moment feels like yesterday. I fell to my knees in my bedroom one morning. I laid my face on the floor and crying out to God to please take the hurt away. I told Him that I was in too much pain. I needed Him to take it away, to heal me, and relieve the suffering and negative emotions. And God responded, saying, "Okay, but you must work with Me." I was confused at first thinking, 'I thought you were going to just take it away?'

Often, we wait on God, but God is waiting for '*Our*' participation. We need Him, but He needs us to position ourselves to receive what He has for us. Like I tell our young people, "There are rules to this!" We must be active participants in our 'Healing Process.' What does that mean?

It means resetting your emotional database. I went through a full emotional detox. How? By realizing every emotion is attached to a thought. I had to see how my '*Thoughts*' had my '*Emotions*' wacky. So, I began to scrutinize '*Every*' thought I had during the day and re-place it with a positive version of that same thought. I also began to put into practice what I like to call "Channel Thinking" by making a list of experiences that impacted me negatively. I would pick one and purposefully think about it from beginning to end. I know this may sound draining, but I began channeling my thinking to focus on the positive impact situations had on me, and how I could use that experience to better my life.

> **'Eboni' Wisdom**
> Every challenge or traumatic experience has a positive element that has contributed to making you better in some way, shape or form.

After weeks of going through my list, when done, I felt liberated, empowered, rejuvenated, free, healed, and even thankful that I survived the trauma. The process helped me to take each experience and allow it to motivate me. I no longer allowed *'the thing'* to hold me back. Most importantly, I felt like a *'Victor'* instead of a *'Victim.'* I understood the scripture when it commands us to "put away childish things." I believe that the scripture says, *"put away"* and not *"throwaway"* for a reason. When we put things away, we *properly place them* where they belong. That is exactly what I did with my childhood hurts.

> "When I was a child, I spoke and thought and reasoned as a child. But when I grew up, I put away childish things."
> — 1 Corinthians 13:11 NLT

Unresolved hurt can cause us to forfeit being and having all that God has created for us. Therefore, be encouraged to confront your hurts, so they will not fester and grow. You do not want to be another *Hurt Person who is Hurting People.*

WALL #2 – FORGIVENESS

I believe it is safe to say that one cannot 'properly' deal with hurt without going through the process of forgiveness. So, let's talk about Forgiveness! Many people get stuck in this area because it's easy to channel our hurt positively. However, it's a bit more difficult to forgive those who have participated in the offense—especially when dealing with an offender who seems to have purposefully set out to hurt us. There is always the conflict; should we forgive these persons or not. Somehow, we have convinced ourselves that if we forgive these individuals, we are "letting them off the hook." Today, I want you to be free and know that this train of thought is far from true! The truth is, complete healing from hurt cannot come unless you wholeheartedly forgive and put all of 'forgiveness's relatives out of your house. Remember, I stated before my issue of the relatives?

> "Let all bitterness and wrath and anger and clamor [perpetual animosity, resentment, strife, fault-finding] and slander be put away from you, along with every kind of malice [all spitefulness, verbal abuse, malevolence]. Be kind and helpful to one another, tender-hearted [compassionate, understanding], forgiving one another [readily and freely], just as God in Christ also forgave you."
> – Ephesians 4:31-32 AMP

So, what is the first step to forgiveness? Well, in my opinion, you must start by deciding to forgive. I know that may sound trivial, but forgiveness is truly a decision. We forgive who we want when we want to forgive them. And the people we choose not to forgive, we don't. Personally, it took me a while to admit the truth of this statement. However, the more I examined my life, the more I began to see for myself. I looked at some people who I continuously forgave, then others who have offended me in the same matter and decided I was *never* going to forgive them.

In my experience, it was easier for me to forgive those who were closest to me because those relationships matter to me the most. Whereas people who were not as close, I decided not to forgive them because they just "didn't matter." For others, your reasoning might be in reverse. Wherever you find yourself, *forgiveness* starts with a decision. Therefore, you should decide to forgive everyone, because ultimately *Forgiveness is For You*! Yes, I decided to forgive everyone who offended me in the past, present, and who will offend me in the future. It is the best thing *For Me*!! Forgiveness is a lifestyle, and one of the keys to success.

Success comes through relationships. A successful life needs successful relationships; successful relationships require a level of intimacy. Unforgiveness is an *'Intimacy Blocker.'* Unforgiveness hardens your heart and prevents people from connecting with you because they cannot see or feel your genuineness. Have you ever met a person and said they seem nice, but something about them is off; you just can't figure what it is? In most instances, you are picking up on the dysfunctions that were created by unforgiveness.

'Eboni' Wisdom

Unforgiveness is a 'Spirit,' and it is not God's will for us to live with something that grows, eventually consumes, hardens our hearts, and infects our motives.

Eventually, your decision making will be tainted. I pray you are beginning to see like I did the importance of making a conscious decision to *Forgive*. Once I realized that unforgiveness would have such a crucial effect on *my life*, I decided that I would not let anyone offend me, and then *control* my destiny through unforgiveness. Only God will *Control My Destiny*!

Deciding to live a lifestyle of forgiveness was only the beginning. In my prayer time, I asked Holy Spirit what I should pray for to help me forgive. Soon after, I began to pray for God to allow me to see my offender the way *He Sees My Offender*. I began to see how brokenhearted they were, and their inability to love and show compassion because they never received love or compassion. I began to empathize with them and understand the pain they must have endured. I saw the statement "hurting people hurt people" as truth.

'Eboni' Wisdom

Expecting a hurt person not to hurt you is like expecting a person with a cold not to cough or sneeze. It's almost impossible! If you're a hurt person, the natural response is to hurt someone else, consciously or unconsciously!

Empathy and praying for what ailed them became my assignment. You may think, 'EB, I'm not there yet!' No worries, keep praying, and meditating on God's Word, and you will be there before you know it. The more time you spend with God, the more you begin to think, talk, and have the same desires He has.

Reflective Moment

Prayer and meditating on God's Word helped me to forgive my father and I saw him as God did.

Again, we reunited when I was 27. Although I decided to forgive him, it took a while to work through the process of releasing all the negative thoughts and emotions I had towards him. By seeing him the way God saw him, I was able to make leaps in my heart. For a moment, I put myself in his shoes. I no longer saw the situation from my point of view, and it was no longer about *me*. What happened to me while he wasn't around, how I felt, or even how much it hurt me didn't matter anymore. The focus shifted, and the situation was about the hurting, broken, scared, lonely, and confused teenager who found himself becoming a father at the age of 19. He didn't know who he was. Because of the hurt, pain, and rejection he felt from his loved ones, he looked for an escape. In efforts to be accepted and fit in, he started engaging in "recreational drugs" and got a hold of a substance that was so much bigger and stronger than him. Before he knew it, he was using any and every drug he could get his hands on. For over 20 years, he was an addict. Who plans to be an addict? You never heard a child say, "When I grow up, I want to be an addict." So, I continued praying to see him through the eyes of Christ, and I began to understand his journey more. I fell in love with my father's heart toward me, instead of hating him for his inability to be there for me.

I no longer penalized him but *appreciated* him for leaving me in the loving arms of my mother. He knew that he was in a toxic state and decided that staying away was the best thing he could do for me. I came to a place where I resolved that my father did the best he could do at the time. It is not my place to judge his decision, but to make peace with his decision. Through constant meditation and prayer, I found peace in *gratitude* for all the things that God protected me from, in my father's absence. I am no longer *bitter*! I will talk more in the next chapter about how my father and I were able to build a loving relationship, but let's continue with forgiveness.

Like I stated, forgiveness is a process. Next, I began to realize that I not only needed to forgive my offender, but I needed to forgive *myself*. Some people may say, well, I didn't do anything wrong. However, I think there's always something we need to take ownership of in our offenses. Even when angered at myself over a situation, I have always found a reason to forgive myself, no matter what the offense. Lastly, I verbally confessed every day (naming my offenders by their names) during my prayer time. I would literally say, "I forgive _____." As we know, the scripture tells us that death and life are in the power of the tongue (Proverbs 18:21). We can speak negatively or positively, but we will have what we 'SAY.' The more I confessed my forgiveness, the more I began to forgive my offenders one by one. Eventually, I was free!

> **'Eboni' Wisdom**
> When you first begin to confess forgiveness, it may be coming out of your mouth, long before you *feel it*. That's okay! Forgiveness is a *Learned Behavior*, **not** a feeling. It is a *Lifestyle*.

Your life will change for the better if you choose to live a lifestyle of forgiveness today! It has been one of the best decisions I have ever made.

WALL #3 – KNOWING WHO YOU ARE

The more John and I talk to people both young and mature, we see a common theme; many people do not know who they are. I always ask the question, "If you were introducing yourself to me, who would you say you are?" Most of the time, we get answers like, I am a mother, father, wife, husband, CEO, supervisor, pastor, deacon, etc. All these things are great but do not define you as a person. It only defines the many hats you wear and the things you do. We are so much more than the titles we have, and the "hats" we wear. In fact, all the great things we do should reflect the great individuals we are.

> **'Eboni' Wisdom**
> "Don't just focus on doing great things, **Be** a great person, and **Greatness** will naturally come out of you."

To be great, I knew I had to work on myself. This part of my self-work was intense because I had to dig down deep and search my soul to find out, "Who is EB?" I pray that by me sharing my journey, you also will be encouraged to discover *Who You Are*.

First, you will never discover who you are without knowing who God is. So, I began to study the characteristics of God. The most important thing I learned about God is that *HE IS LOVE*.

> "The one who does not love has not become acquainted with God [does not and never did know Him], for God is love. [He is the originator of love, and it is an enduring attribute of His nature.]"
> – 1 John 4:8 AMP

Knowing that one of God's characteristics is love helped me see because He is my creator, everything that He possesses *I Also* possess. Why? I was created in His Image. Then I went further and thought if God is Love then, what does the Bible say about love? In chapter 13 of 1 Corinthians, the Bible clearly breaks down the definition of love.

"Love endures with patience and serenity, love is kind and thoughtful, and is not jealous or envious; love does not brag and is not proud or arrogant. It is not rude; it is not self-seeking; it is not provoked [nor overly sensitive and easily angered]; it does not consider a wrong endured. It does not rejoice at injustice but rejoices with the truth [when right and truth prevail]. Love bears all things [regardless of what comes], believes all things [looking for the best in each one], hopes all things [remaining steadfast during difficult times], endures all things [without weakening].

> Love never fails [it never fades nor ends]. But as for prophecies, they will pass away; as for tongues, they will cease; as for the gift of special knowledge, it will pass away. And now there remain: faith [abiding trust in God and His promises], hope [confident expectation of eternal salvation], love [unselfish love for others growing out of God's love for me], these three [the choicest graces]; but the greatest of these is love."
> – 1 Corinthians 13:4-8, 13 AMP

You may feel like I did the first time I read this scripture. I said to myself, 'wow, I am more messed up than I thought.' If I am created in

God's image, then I should have a lot more in common with Him! No worries buddy; you're a great person!

Holy Spirit began to share with me that *I Do* possess *All* the same qualities as God! However, I must concentrate on the characteristics that are weak and strengthen them. These characteristics reside on the inside of all of us; we must grow and mature in them. Remember, we are all a work in progress, but it is important to stay in the flow of *Working*! Now there are so many GREAT characteristics of God. The more I looked at who He is, it helped me to identify who I am. So, this is how it works. God has all these great characteristics that He possesses, and then He says that *He Created Us In His Image*. Knowing this makes it clear and gives us an understanding of who *GOD* says we are. HE is the only one who can *Define You*. Why? Because He is the only one that is *qualified* to do so, "*He Did That!*" The best thing about letting God define us, whether we are aware of it or not, these characteristics are still the *Complete* definition of who we are because God put them in us. Listen, if you see a car parked on the street, not turned on, or moving, does that not make it a car? It is still a car! No one has turned it on, and it's not moving yet. This example applies to some of us. We may not be turned on in every area, and moving as we should, but that's ok. We are still *everything* God says we are! We are doing our self-work, and soon we will be functioning at our highest level of performance.

> "Then God said, "Let Us (Father, Son, Holy Spirit) make man in Our image, according to Our likeness [not physical, but a spiritual personality and moral likeness]; and let them have complete authority over the fish of the sea, the birds of the air, the cattle, and over the entire earth, and over everything that creeps and crawls on the earth. So, God created man in His own image, in the image and likeness of God He created him; male and female He created them."
> – Genesis 1:26-27 AMP

After studying these characteristics, I began to see that I am an ambitious, brilliant, caring, consistent, creative, empathetic, focused, grounded, honest, humble, kind, loving, nurturing, one of a kind, purpose-driven, reliable, strong, supportive, talented, trustworthy, and unstoppable

Woman, who possesses the ability to make her dreams come true because the *Greater One* lives on the inside of me!

The next thing, Holy Spirit led me to do was to identify my gifts and talents. Most of the time, you can identify your gifts and talents by identifying the things you love to do. It may be singing, or writing, dancing, or drawing, creating movies, or public speaking. Some people are gifted in areas they overlook, like having excellent organizational skills, or the ability to be a team leader. These are all gifts and talents that also help us identify who we are. We began to learn what we like and dislike. We learn what we want and do not want to do. We also figure out the direction we want to take in life. With confidence, discovering *Who You Are* becomes clearer.

I remember feeling insecure and like I was a circle trying to fit in a square peg everywhere I went. From the age of 15 up to 27, I was unsure about who I was. "Anti-social," people said, "Oh, she's stuck up." They couldn't see it was simply me not feeling good about myself. Not knowing who you are is equivalent to you placing objects into a huge bag that has a hole in the bottom. *It Will Never Be Full!* People can give you compliments, accolades, acknowledgments, encouragement, support, etc. Until you get the revelation of who you are, through your relationship with God, consider yourself as 'the bag' possessing the inability to *Be Filled*.

Notice I keep using the word "*Be.*" My definition of "*BE*" represents the past, present, and future. It also represents me remaining in a consistent state of knowing who I am, without ignoring the past hurt, pain, and obstacles I've walked through. Moreover, understanding that I am much more than my struggles. I appreciate them because they've contributed to the person I am today. Confidently knowing that my future is predestined, and as I keep my focus on God, making sure I am positioning myself, *I Will* walk in everything He has planned for me to *BE* and do. Every day, I am *Excited* that I am *Becoming* who God Created me to *Be*. This makes me *Complete AND Whole*!

The most important thing is to take the information you learn about yourself and understand it. Because of whom God created you to be, know that *You Are Valuable*! God created you *uniquely*, and you have something to give that this world is waiting to receive. Your uniqueness is what draws people to you. Just like recipes have ingredients, so does this world. We are the ingredients of this world. The Bible even refers to us as the salt of the earth (Mathew 5:13), which is why you need to be yourself. When we all focus on who we are and become who God created us to be, we will complete the recipe that God formulated for this world.

Remember, God took His time and gifted you with individual gifts and talents. One of the best gifts you can give back to Him is to *Use* your gifts and talents to be the *Best You Can Be*. Shine! The world is waiting for *You*!

> "Let your light shine before men in such a way that they may see your good deeds and moral excellence, and [recognize and honor and] glorify your Father who is in heaven."
> – Matthew 5:16 AMP

WALL #4 – PURPOSE

I believe this word is the most common question that John and I have come across in our conversations with people. No matter what cultural background, race, or economic status, people are lost when they can't figure out what their purpose is. No matter where you find yourself in life, your soul will always long to fulfill your God-given purpose.

When questions come, I find there is a general answer that will lead to your specific answer. Above all things, we were created to bring *Glory* and *Honor to God* with our lives; and to worship Him through our lifestyle. We were created to lead people to Christ by living a godly life. We should display that God is real, and *His Principles Work*. We were created to be a representation of Christ in His absence.

Were you ever in a classroom as a child and were chosen as the teacher's assistant? When I was in elementary school, the students had to vote. If you wanted consideration for "Class President" you had to run for office. Well, I did that and was president twice during my elementary school years. "Class President" meant you were second-in-command. You assisted the teacher by taking some of her responsibilities, such as marking spelling tests, quizzes, and handing out paperwork. Also, I reported students who weren't complying with the class rules, etc. Most importantly, when the teacher stepped out of the room, but she could still hear and see what was going on, I was the "teacher." The class president *performed* in an *authoritative position* until the teacher physically returned.

Did you know it is '*Your Purpose In The Earth*,' to perform in Christ's authoritative position until He physically returns? Our purpose is to walk in His power, study His word, believe it, obey it, and receive it in our hearts. We are to speak it out of our mouths and live a life that lines up with our confession. To walk in healing, integrity, godly character, kindness, temperance, meekness, humbleness, I can go on and on. Above all else, we are to *Walk In Love,* which leads us to a lifestyle of *purpose*. No matter what we choose to do, it should be based on the goal of pleasing God with our lives. Our purpose is to be like Christ!

> "I assure you and most solemnly say to you, anyone who believes in Me [as Savior] will also do the things that I do, and he will do even greater things than these [in extent and outreach], because I am going to the Father. And I will do whatever you ask in My name [as My representative], this I will do, so that the Father may be glorified and celebrated in the Son. If you ask Me anything in My name [as My representative], I will do it. "If you [really] love Me, you will keep and obey My commandments."
> — John 14:12-15 AMP

After receiving an overall revelation of purpose and beginning to walk in it, identifying my specific purpose was easy. This is where all four walls in this chapter work together. I took the time to do my self-work and deal with the *hurt*, learn how to *forgive, discover* who *I am*, and identify my gifts and talents. I began to see all the work I put in would help me to help others to experience the freedom, joy, and peace that I experience daily. God's specific purpose for me is to take my gifts and talents and operate in them, cultivate them, and then use them to bring others to Christ. For example, I've always 'Loved' playing in people's hair as a child. I loved to wash, comb, and style it. I even loved the smells of the different chemicals, creams, and sprays while at the salon with my mother. I began to do my mom's hair from start to finish at the age of 12. I gave her full relaxers and styled it in a very popular hairstyle called a "French Roll." I did my neighbors hair, friends' hair, and even my relatives' hair all through my teenage years. I found comfort and fun in doing hair. I was happy on the inside and allowed to be creative. I enjoyed doing hair!

By the time I graduated from high school, it was a no brainer. I told my mom I wanted to go to hair school to be a Cosmetologist, and she supportively agreed. When I earned my license and initially started working, I was around 20. Like many, I had no clue what my *purpose* was. Around 25, I began doing self-work. I prayed to God, asking for help to find my purpose. As my clients came to get their hair done, they began to talk to me and share personal situations. I began to share with them, encourage, comfort, and pray for them. I shared scriptures they could meditate on to help them get through those hard times. I was still learning and growing myself, but God had a plan.

Women began to say, "Wow, not only are you a great hairdresser; you're a great mentor." At first, I would laugh and say, "Girl, I'm just talking." They began to express to me the hope they felt after our conversations and no longer wanted to give up. Our exchange motivated them to fight and make it through their challenges. They even shared how they were challenged to grow and become better people, not only for them but for their children, families, and loved ones. And then it hit me, I had an overwhelming feeling that spoke to me, and Holy Spirit said, "This is your purpose." Wow! Before I knew it, I was using my talent of doing hair to lead me into using my gift of mentoring people. Eventually, God gave me the idea of Mentoring for Success Organization. Today, John and I not only hold monthly group, couple, and one to one sessions, but we visit shelters and provide *mentoring sessions* for the homeless, that ultimately lead people to Christ. This was one example of an area that purpose has led me to.

I genuinely believe by me sharing this, you too will walk in your *purpose*. You will find, although you have one purpose, the manifestation will develop through the different gifts and talents that God has given you. But God, in His infinite wisdom, makes them all sync and work together.

Sometimes we let the word 'purpose' overwhelm us, but I encourage you to keep it *simple*. Use the nuggets I've provided for you in this chapter. If unsure, I pray that God will reveal all things to you soon.

"You have not chosen Me, but I have chosen you, and I have appointed and placed and purposefully planted you, so that you would go and bear fruit and keep on bearing, and that your fruit will remain and be lasting, so that whatever you ask of the Father in My name [as My representative] He may give to you. This [is what] I command you: that you love and unselfishly seek the best for one another."

– John 15:16-17 AMP

CHAPTER II –
THE 4 WALLS OF THE FAMILY

Family is something most of us have, whether we like them or not. Many of us can identify with the work it takes to keep our families strong, peaceful, and together, where we can all get along, create memories, and grow in love together. Also, at some point, we have experienced the struggle of creating family boundaries without offending each other or becoming combative. Ultimately, we should be able to develop a healthy family dynamic that we are proud to pass down to the next generation. The best thing we can give our family is a strong legacy to be proud of. So how do we create this *Healthy* family?

In this chapter, I will discuss the four walls I believe will help you to create a strong foundation for your family through *Communication*, *Transparency*, *Accountability,* and *Unity*. In John and my personal experience, and now as we mentor families, we have found by strengthening these four walls, families have become empowered, unified, and able to support each other through any and every situation. By using these four walls as principles, you will see your family transform for the better. In chapter I, we worked through the four walls of the heart. Now you are well equipped to work on the four walls of your family. So, let's get started!

WALL #1 – COMMUNICATION

When we think about the word 'communication,' the word 'talk' is the first thing that comes to mind. Talking seems simple to do because we do it every and all day; it's a requirement for communicating. However, just because you're talking doesn't mean you are *communicating*. The art of it goes far beyond talking and requires you to be in tune with what you are feeling and trying to convey. If you're not careful, one can easily and heavily affect the other.

Learning how to communicate is necessary. I promised myself that I will always talk, even when it's uncomfortable for me. Some of us are holding back ourselves, and others, simply because we are afraid to do so. Communication begins with self-searching and a settling within you. It's essential to be clear on what you need to convey, as well as why and how you will convey it. Communication requires you to *think* before you *speak*.

Listen, this whole world is controlled by words, and how we communicate. If you have ever attended a school, held a job, been to a hospital, or in a courtroom, you know that your whole life can be changed simply by the communication of authoritative people in these places. Well, it's the same way in your family. You can control, arguments, strife, fighting, and all other types of dysfunctions, by the way you communicate. Doing so in the right manner can help you to support your family emotionally, mentally, and spiritually, especially your children. I'm telling you what I know; I have seen my family turn in the right direction, hearts mended, and situations resolved by exercising healthy talks. If you simply communicate with God, speak His word over your household, and communicate with your family, you will see. You can cancel out depression, suicide, low self-esteem, anger, and anything else that tries to attack you and your loved ones.

Now, if you noticed in the *first chapter*, no matter the situation I am dealing with or issues I am working on, I am always going to go to God first concerning the matter, and *communication* is no different. The first person I learned how to talk to was God. The more I developed my skills with Him, I found that communicating with others has become *quite easy*.

Communication is one of the highest forms of intimacy we will ever experience. Being with God and praying to Him has been my highest form of intimacy thus far. Also, my connection to Him has taught me to speak from my heart and tell Him exactly how I feel. No sugar coating, covering up, half-truths, and no lies. I had to let go of the fear that God would disown me and not love me because of my flaws. Always know that God's love is *unconditional*, which makes Him different from man. He is not shocked by our flaws or shortcomings. He knew everything about us before we were born, and He promised to love us from the womb until we see Him again.

I remember years ago having a moment with God. During my prayer time, I began to tell Him how selfish I was. It may sound weird, but I needed to confess. I realized that most of my reasoning for not doing a lot of things, including some of what He wanted me to do, was because I was a very selfish individual. *I know it's crazy! I was shocked too!* It took me a while to admit, but I knew to acknowledge it would free me. You might be just like me. For a long time, I was unaware of my behavior. I considered myself to be a well-rounded, caring person, and this was true. As long as me caring for you didn't mean I had to sacrifice or be uncomfortable for any length of time, we were good. I wasn't intentionally selfish, but I *was*. Selfishness can be subtle and a hindrance when communicating. When I chose to remain closed off when sharing with others because it made me feel vulnerable and uncomfortable, in essence, I was saying; comfort was more important to me than their feelings and reasons why they needed me to communicate with them. As we know, words have power. We must realize that we can leave people in high levels of distress when we choose not to communicate. The ability to talk is a privilege, and we should do so to the best of our ability.

> "Anxiety in a man's heart weighs it down,
> But a good (encouraging) word makes it glad."
> – Proverbs 12:25 AMP

'Eboni' Wisdom

Ultimately God holds us responsible for every word we speak. He wants us to use wisdom, self-control, and discernment when doing so. Our words are to be used to build up, strengthen, and support one another, even in challenging times.

> "Do not let unwholesome [foul, profane, worthless, vulgar] words ever come out of your mouth, but only such speech as is good for building up others, according to the need and the occasion, so that it will be a blessing to those who hear [you speak]."
> – Ephesians 4:29 AMP

Priceless! That is the best way to describe how His unconditional love makes me feel when I openly communicate with God. I feel relieved, and like a huge weight is lifted off me. In my journey to overcome selfishness, I sensed overwhelming support from Holy Spirit. I knew that He would be patient and help me as I worked to get rid of my selfish ways. The same way I opened to God made me realize that communication with my family would require this same level of honesty.

'Eboni' Wisdom

Honesty is absolutely, a necessary part of communication. It's important you be honest with God, yourself, and then others. I always say "if misunderstanding were a rash *honesty* can definitely *clear it up*."

So how does communication work within the family? I began to work on my communication with my husband John first, using the same principles I'm sharing with you in this chapter. Once we got that ball rolling, we decided to implement this practice into our family, starting with the people we live with.

We have three beautiful girls Jadé, Jaelyn, and Janiya, who are ages 24, 19, and 16. They are all the most brilliant, talented, creative, gifted creatures I've ever met. Spoken like a true mother! But really, we're blessed to have them, and I am honored to be called their Mom. With that said, they also have three different personalities. So, we noticed that if we wanted to introduce healthy communication to the girls, we needed to work on creating an atmosphere that was conducive to how they communicate. This is particularly important!

'Eboni' Wisdom
Sometimes families struggle with communication simply because there is a tendency to jump into conversations without preparing all family members for the conversation.

We sat our girls down and said we need to talk. We established time would be set aside at least once a month to have family meetings. During the meetings, we took the time to communicate our feelings on whatever we need to talk about with each other. Most importantly, we created a new atmosphere in our home of a "Judge Free Zone." No judging, looking down, dishonoring, or disrespecting each other because of our difference. We agreed to always put ourselves in each other's shoes and show empathy, especially if we came to a point where we couldn't agree. We've decided we will *agree to disagree*.

The girls loved it! Among other things, they felt it was okay to have a voice even though they were our children. They each felt comfortable sharing their opinions and were able to communicate openly and honestly. We noticed meeting after meeting, the more we talked with the girls, the more they wanted to communicate with us. The most challenging part of communicating with our children has been learning to exercise *patience*. Although we have different personalities, the five of us are incredibly passionate people. Often, we noticed impatience with one another when working with each other and during the process of communication. Initially, we had to learn not to over talk one another, but listen and wait for our turn to speak. When we first began having our family meetings, we used an object to pass around as a visual. The object was a reminder not to speak unless we were holding the object. The process may sound juvenile, but it worked! Patience is truly a virtue and a vital part of communication. What helps me with patience? Putting myself in the shoes of the other person, and it makes me focus on their perspective rather than wanting them to hurry up and agree with my perspective. Furthermore, patience helped me to see their needs and made me want to work with them to come up with a resolution.

Communication is like a window. If you are willing to open the window and stick your neck out, you can see there are so many other ways to view a thing. That doesn't always mean you will want to change your view, but you won't know its surety until you consider looking from another angle. I believe communication is a principle to continually work on improving. As a family, we have grown and matured in this area. We talk about *everything*, from sex to education, spiritual growth, including our monthly goals, yearly goals, and life goals. John and I also share our past experiences and future goals. At times, we allow them to give us advice as we provide them with instruction and create boundaries. Even though we are still the parents, we can have an exchange. During our times of reprimand, I always start by asking the question, "If I was your daughter, and you were my mother, what would you do in this situation?" My purpose is to help them understand that we are not trying to be mean parents; we just want what's best for them. And to show, one day they will want what is best for their children. Communication has taken my family to another level of agreement and given us a better understanding of each other's specific needs. Our new way has helped us to support one another accordingly.

WALL #2 – TRANSPARENCY

Transparency can be uncomfortable. Although I mentioned honesty earlier, transparency is a bit more than being honest. Honesty is based on me telling the truth, but transparency includes me allowing you to see how I feel about that truth and how it has or is affecting me. It's more of allowing my emotional side to be seen.

John and I talk to a lot of parents who have said that they don't think that it's necessary to be transparent with their children. They feel like sharing their feelings and showing emotion in front of their children, is a sign of *weakness*. Well, I was also raised with that same way of thinking. Still, as I began to explore different methods to become closer to my girls and build a strong family, I can wholeheartedly say that transparency has been effective and beneficial in my family relationships. I have shared some very personal experiences with my children. For example:

I believe Jadé was about 15 years old when she began her menstrual cycle. I knew that it was time for us to have a conversation about sex with her. Now, John and I both started having sex around the same age, and we knew that we wanted better for our children. We even said to each other, wouldn't it be great if we could raise our children with the *godly* principle of remaining *virgins* until marriage. So, we prayed together and asked God to give us creative ways to communicate with our girls on the importance of saving themselves for marriage. I'll never forget the family meeting. John and I were so nervous. We never had to have this type of talk before. John began talking to them from a guy's point of view, and I heard a whisper in my ear say, "*Be Transparent*," just tell them your experience."

I remember feeling my stomach drop to my toes. I said to myself, but what are they going to think about me? I'm their *mother*! As I looked into their eyes and saw three innocent souls looking to me with a level of dependence I had never felt before, my love for them superseded the fear and shame I felt. So, I opened my mouth and began to share with them how I gave up my virginity at the age of 15, to a boy I thought loved me. I eventually found out the whole time I was with him; he was betraying me by seeing other girls. I shared with my daughters how I felt, the reasons why I had sex, and the reasons why I regretted doing it. I also expressed how I didn't concentrate on blaming the young man; I only focused on taking ownership of my actions, forgiving myself, and being a better person for *me*.

Now, am I saying that we should just tell our children everything? No, but if your child is up against a situation you have already been through, it's most beneficial to be transparent and share your experience with them.

It's natural for human beings to need to connect with others, especially during difficult times in our lives. Your children are no different. Isn't this why Jesus came from heaven to earth to show us how to live? He wanted to experience what we experience and feel what we feel (hurt, betrayal, etc.). He was willing so that He could have a deeper connection with us and prove it's possible to live a Christian lifestyle on earth. Now when we go to Him in prayer, we can't say to Him, "Jesus, you don't understand." He not only understands us, but He experienced our hurts and *more*!

> ### Reflective Moment
> The transparency developed inside our home equipped me to communicate with my extended family, outside the home, especially with my biological father.

I shared a little about my father in the first chapter. After working through the hurt, and embracing the process of forgiveness, I realized that building a relationship with him would take work, communication, and transparency. Initially, I had reservations about building a relationship with him. If your parent has ever hurt you, you are tempted not to want a relationship with them at all. Through prayer and meditation, I learned to resist those feelings and go into the relationship with a mindset of accepting my father at whatever stage he was in his life. I had to create a "Judge Free Zone" between us. We had intimate talks about his childhood, which helped me to understand him better. We also discussed regular day to day struggles and his medical challenges. He was hilarious, so we always laughed, joked, and became very friendly. We also connected on a spiritual level. We came to a place where he would call me to pray for him, and we exchanged scriptures for encouragement.

My father developed lung cancer. One day he was at work having an extremely difficult time breathing. He called me and said, "I want you to pray with me *right now.*" I prayed with him, and immediately through God's power, his breathing calmed down. That day was the day I realized we did it! My father and I beat the odds of having an estranged relationship. We were able to form a bond despite the obstacles of the past. We accepted each other for who we were. Don't get me wrong, there were some awkward moments, and sometimes he would say things I didn't particularly like. But I would tell him, "Hey pop, I don't like it when you say things like that." and he would say, "Ok, ok, ok." We learned how to have the conversations we *needed* and to leave unnecessary discussions alone. Creating a bond was more important to us.

When my father became terminally ill, he asked me to come and visit him. John and I arrived in the city he lived in, and he immediately asked us to go to a doctor's appointment with him. To this day, I believe he planned for the day to go that way. I will never forget the out of body experience I had sitting there while his doctor told us my father only had *days to live*. I believed he knew, but he didn't know how to tell me. I can still see the look in his eyes, and it's making me emotional right now as I am writing. The look on his face said he had given up, but he didn't want our relationship to end. The hurt I felt in my heart was excruciating. I had never felt that kind of loss before. I felt like my heart was being ripped out of my chest. The pain was different, unexplainable. I was losing the first man I ever loved. As I tried to convince him to stay in *Faith, to Believe God's word*, I reminded him that people had received news from doctors before, and they are alive, doing well, and still living to tell their story.

He told me that he was tired of fighting with cancer and would rather be with Jesus. We cried together that day. As always, amid our tears, we were in the car, and John was driving us back to his place. My dad was seated right behind me, and he grabbed my shoulder as I was still crying hysterically. With his joking self, he tells me, "*Stop Crying Baby, I Gotta Go, Gotta Go, Gotta Go!*"! I rolled my eyes at him and told him, "*Pop, That's Not Funny, You Play Too Much!*"

We kept laughing and crying. When we arrived at his house, he went into his bedroom. It took me an hour or so to collect myself. With amazing support from my husband, I was able to go into the room. We were in there alone, and that was the last time we had our most intimate and transparent conversation. We discussed things that were important to him. He shared more details about his life, who he was, and how he had ended up in his position. He also mentioned his struggle with loneliness and fear from a child of being alone. He told me that there was no one to blame for what he was going through; he did it to himself by abusing his body from a young age. He shared with me repeatedly how much he loved me.

I found out he had signed himself into rehab during one of the times we lost communication. He did that on the 28th day in April, which is my birthday. He said that since the day I was born, I was always on his mind, and he thought about me *every* single day. I could go on and on with the details of our conversation. I learned so much. If he never taught me anything, that day, he taught me how to be a *Hero*. He wanted me to help him pick out his outfit to wear to *his* funeral, from the suit, shirt, the tie, handkerchief, socks, and shoes. He asked John to come into the room and help. As I stood there, we laughed about our love for shoes, and he tried to pick out the flashiest ones, as I told him they didn't match. He began to thank John for always taking great care of me. He told my husband he appreciated him being there for me, even when he couldn't. He encouraged John to keep being the great father and husband that he could be. In his favorite words, he told John for the last time, *"Take Care Of My Baby."* He reassured me that he was ok and wasn't afraid to die, but I could see the fear in his eyes. That day I watched my father go through every emotion of happiness, sadness, silliness, regret, fear, and even anger. I felt so helpless because I wanted to relieve him of his emotional pain and couldn't.

Reflective Moment

Looking back now, my being there was more than enough. He knew he wasn't alone, and he felt comfortable enough with me, to be TRANSPARENT about everything he was feeling.

After a few days of visiting with him, it was time for us to return home. I felt like he knew it would be our last time seeing each other. In his efforts to keep me hopeful, he talked about us coming back soon to celebrate our birthdays together.

We talked on the phone every day after I returned home. Eventually, because of Lung Cancer, his voice became a whisper, and it was hard to hear him over the phone. About a month later, I received a call stating my father transitioned. Although I thought I had prepared myself, I don't think you can ever be. However, I cried tears of *Joy* because he was no longer suffering, and I remembered all the times we laughed, talked, prayed, read scripture, and cracked jokes *together*.

I often like to share this story of how powerful transparency can be. I think it proves when you are willing to open up and be vulnerable with your loved ones, the reward can be *great, bring healing, and be powerful*. My father's openness gave me the strength I needed to *grieve properly*. It is truly a testimony of what transparency can do, and I am grateful to have conquered my fear and learn of its power.

Now that we have gone over '*Communication*' and '*Transparency*,' let's move on to our next principle.

WALL #3 – ACCOUNTABILITY

Accountability is a touchy topic. We all have our preconceived ideas about how far we should go when it comes to being accountable. I've heard people use excuses like "I'm Grown," implying that they are not to be treated like a child when asked to be accountable.

Accountability must start with the proper mindset so it can be viewed as a positive and not negative. It's a simple principle that holds much weight and can have a positive effect on your family, just as it has mine.

Initially, John and I thought that accountability was unnecessary. We have learned that it is *highly necessary*. Children must be accountable to their parents, but in my opinion, it's even more important that parents be accountable to their children. You may think, 'Okay EB, why is accountability so important?' First and foremost, it's for safety reasons. My husband developed a rule in our household, which says, "Everybody knows where everybody goes." When you think about all the crazy things that happen in the world, and how quickly things can change in one day, it is *safe* for everyone in the household to be aware of each other's whereabouts. Therefore, we developed a family group chat on our phones. As we all travel to our different destinations, we text the group our various locations throughout the day. Yes, that includes my husband, and I. God forbid if there is a tragedy or destruction, we will know whether one of us has been affected or not.

On a deeper level, we require accountability to one another with what we need to work on within ourselves, attitudes, and behaviors. We adjust, improve our weaknesses, and work on our individual and collective goals established in our family meetings. Accountability has helped us to stay focused, away from distractions, and avoid getting off track. It's easy to keep your kids focused when you commit to staying focused on them.

I've found the only thing that has stood between accountability, and I was *pride*. Anyone who struggles with accountability may want to check their bag of pride. Most of us carry pride around but need to make sure the bag remains *empty*.

Being accountable doesn't minimize you. In fact, it proves you to be a very mature person. Though appearing unnecessary at first, I am a witness to the bond accountability develops with your children and the appreciation that will happen from your willingness to be accountable to them. The implementation of it also breeds stability, which is what children want and need. No child likes to wonder if you're going to do what you said or if you're going to show up when you promised to be there. This type of wondering only adds stress to your kids' lives and causes them to look to other people, and even their peers for accountability.

'Eboni' Wisdom

We as parents cannot expect our children to *respect* and *honor* us when we are not willing to be accountable. Your children can respect you because of the position you hold in their lives as a parent, but never have a healthy relationship with you. However, when they *honor* you, they will esteem you highly and have a special place in their hearts, because they value you. They will look to *you* for love, support, stability, etc. And, they are *willing* to return those things back to you, without any reservations.

When we teach this principle, our children learn what's expected at school, extracurricular activities, and life. Failing to teach this principle has the consequence of them struggling and not knowing how to be a man or woman of their word. Accountability helps them grow and gives them the confidence to know that throughout their lives they will stand out, be recognized, advance quickly, and be successful just because they understand, and operate in, the principle of *accountability*.

"Therefore, rejecting all falsehood [whether lying, defrauding, telling half-truths, spreading rumors, any such as these], SPEAK TRUTH EACH ONE WITH HIS NEIGHBOR, for we are all parts of one another [and we are all parts of the body of Christ]."
— Ephesians 4:25 AMP

WALL #4 – UNITY

Unity is one of my favorite topics because it's something that John and I fought for at the beginning of our marriage. Now, it comes naturally. Unity is not only about doing things together, but it is a *mindset*. I have seen a lot of marriages fail because of a blind notion; they believe that if they did certain things together or were able to work well together, they've experienced unity. Sadly, the couple discovers years later how disconnected they are from each other. Listen, being able to run a business, complete home improvement projects, buy properties, or even function in the home together does not mean you have *Unity*.

The definition of *Unity* is developing a spirit of oneness, by coming together, using God's principles to define what your purpose is as a family. Let's be clear, your family could consist of just you and your spouse living in the house, which is defined as family. Unity must start with the immediate family members who are living under the same roof before it can spill over into your extended family, and others.

During the early stages of our marriage, we realized that we thoroughly enjoyed each other's company. Even in our dating stages, we pretty much did everything together. We developed a friendship first and became "mad cool" before we started dating. I don't know if we realized it, but looking back, we were *best friends* before we married. Fortunately, because of the work we put into our marriage, our friendship is solid and amazing.

Initially, when we married, we moved in with his parents, with plans to be there for one year. That is precisely what we did. A year later, we found our first apartment in the area close to both of our parents. We thought to function together, on our own, would be a no-brainer, because we are *so close*. I mean, anyone who knows us until this day will say, "When you see John, you see Eboni." We are truly inseparable. Now don't think we cannot function without each other. John goes to work daily, and so would I. I have been a stay at home mom for 16 years now, and we have no problems handling our responsibilities separately. However, we make a conscious decision to do the bulk of our running around *together,* for we genuinely enjoy each other's company.

Now here's the thing, when we moved into the apartment, we began to see that although we were together all the time, we struggled with being *unified.* John had his ideas, goals, and plans for us as a family, and so did I. He also had his thoughts, and ways, of exactly how we were going to achieve those goals. Well, we immediately began to bump heads in different areas of our marriage. It seemed like we could not agree on anything; we struggled in coming together in our finances, how we should run our daily affairs, making decisions for us, and even in communication. We were *always* together doing things but had no *Unity.* We began to become very frustrated but realized we had to sit down and have conversation(s) to develop unity between one another. During those talks, we had to identify the goals for *our* marriage. John would express what he thought our goals should be, and I would do the same. With a little compromise and a lot of flexibility, we were able to choose *our* goals, form ideas together, and come up with plans that worked for both of us. A lot of people say it's not that simple. They ask us how do we do it. Our answer is *always,* "Because we *both* are willing." We are consistently willing to be flexible, to give, to be understanding, to empathize with, and to support one another. We are also willing to put down our boxing gloves and stop fighting to be *right* and fight to *become one.* Moreover, we are committed to being on one accord, with one mindset, in *Unity.*

We were now off to a great start, but there was one thing that drastically changed our lives and has remained the thing that keeps us operating in the *Spirit of Unity.* Are you ready! Ok, here it is! A few years later, we were visiting a church (which is now our church), and the Pastor, who is now our Apostle, was teaching on marriage. He began to share that we didn't get married just for us, because we love each other and want to be together for the rest of our lives. He said it's vital for us all to know that *"God Has A Purpose For Your Marriage."* I believe that was one of the *greatest* things we'd ever heard. We had an *"Ahh Hahh"* moment, which immediately changed our thinking forever. When you get the revelation, that God himself has a specific purpose for your marriage, you will realize that you two being together is so much *bigger* than *You!* If you are married, there is a reason why you both should come together as one, emotionally being free to express yourself, and physically being able to support and love each other. Also, it's important to become one mentally. You may ask, "What does that mean EB?" It means we think alike *on purpose*, with a *purpose*.

'Eboni' Wisdom

If married or marriage pending know you are successful together, you grow together, and there is nothing you can't do when you come into agreement. It's not about *Me*, but it's about *Us*.

Above all else, we learned the importance of becoming *Spiritually One* with one accord by praying together, reading scriptures together, and confessing *Bible Promises* over our marriage daily.

When we left the church that day, we came home and began to pray together and ask God to *Unify Us* and to *Help Us* form a stable and unbreakable bond of unity deep down in our spirits. We asked God for forgiveness for not seeing the bigger picture and *His Purpose For Our Marriage*. Most importantly, we submitted ourselves to one another in the spirit of *Unity*, vowing always to come together and pray and ask God to direct us in *all* of our decision makings, so that our marriage would always reflect and represent *His Kingdom*. *That* is the purpose of our marriage and *yours too*. Husbands and wives must be unified so that people can see through our relationship, how we love, support, and treat one another as a reflection of how God loves, supports, and treats us.

The spirit of unity created in our family has caused us to grow seamlessly; we always move in sync with each other. One day, I had a conversation with our girls, and during our talk, each of them was confirming things I had already prayed about. They were quoting the prayers that I privately petitioned to God *Verbatim*! Blown away, it almost brought me to tears to know how we echo each other in the spirit. It's an *awesome* feeling to know that we are on the same page at the same exact time. *It Is Simply Beautiful!*

Marriage was intended to represent God's Love for the church, and a *godly* marriage is the core of a *successful* family, but we will never get there if we don't have *Unity*.

"How good and pleasant it is when God's people
live together in unity!"
— Psalms 133:1NIV

CHAPTER III –
THE 4 WALLS OF THE SOUL

The soul of a man is what I like to call the *Central Station* of every *Human*. It is the headquarters and the source of who we are. This is where it all goes down! Who you are is determined by your soul. Your soul controls your decision making and who you will become in the future is predicted by it. Most importantly, your *Soul* determines your *Spirituality*, what you believe in, who you believe in, and what *Belief System* you choose to live by. In this chapter, I will share four key components that will benefit your soul by discussing *Salvation*, *Renewing your Mind*, a *Progressive Lifestyle*, and *Sacrificing to Serve*. During my journey of self-work, I have found that these four principles have changed my life for the better, given me balance, and helped me to remain focused. I like to refer to these as the four walls of *Strength*.

Now, if you're like me, the *Soul* is not typically discussed in our everyday conversations, if we are out with friends, at lunch with our co-workers, or lounging at home with the family. The topics we randomly discuss usually are not about the soul. However, it is a highly necessary and significant conversation. Although I grew up in and attended church all my life, I can honestly say that I didn't fully understand the importance of the soul's position until I was well into the adult stages of my life. In fact, before then, I didn't know that I should care about my soul. I always thought that if I took care of my spiritual man by praying, reading scriptures, and trying to "live right," everything else would fall in line. Now, I wasn't totally off track because these are some of the necessary ingredients in having a *prosperous soul*, but there was so much more I needed to tap into.

At some point in every person's life, whether you realize it or not, your soul can experience what I like to call a *"Soul-Tantrum."* What I mean is, our souls often can produce a level of uncertainty within us, which causes us to become unclear on our views, form questions in our mind, and bring up questions about our past or present situations that were suppressed. Also, it can cause us to act out, and even present an urgency to make decisions without thinking the results can have a critical effect on our future. In fact, depending on what position your soul is in, you can become frustrated, overwhelmed, and confused all at the same time. *Ask Me How Do I Know?*

I remember my 30th birthday like it was yesterday. John made so many beautiful plans for me, bought me gifts, and arranged a mini-vacation at a five-star hotel not far from home. He took me shopping, scheduled spa time, and bought me two or three cakes during that weekend. He also made reservations for multiple dinners with just he and I, and dinners with the girls, family, and friends. With all these beautiful gestures, it was still one of the saddest birthdays of my life. Leading up to my 30th birthday, I was *So Excited!* I couldn't wait!

However, that morning I sat on my bed's edge, and "my life flashed in front of my eyes." We've all heard that saying before. Immediately, I began to cry, and I asked myself, "What have you done with your life so far, and are you satisfied?"

It's like all through my teenage years and my twenties, this question never crossed my mind. I was just living life, doing whatever made me happy for the day, with the idea that somehow a successful life was just going to come to me. I began to scan my life from beginning up until 30, and to my surprise, I was extremely disappointed. I felt like I needed to be doing more. I began to share my feelings with John as he looked at me with a very puzzled look on his face. He could tell I was terribly upset, but he couldn't figure out *why*. As we talked that morning, we began to make a list of all the accomplishments I had made up until that point. The list included me having done well in my career as a Cosmetologist, being a fantastic stay-at-home mom, providing extra support for the specific needs of our three beautiful daughters. Also, we had met our goals and had been homeowners for two years. He felt like I was a role model for our girls, and was proud of the ways we served at our church, etc. All those things sound good before 30, but on that day, I questioned all of it. At that moment, I felt empty, and instantly the list wasn't enough. I was overwhelmed with feelings of failure. The more I sat there, the more I tried to figure out what I could do to make me feel better about my life. So, I came up with this bright idea to start a *new career*! I felt like I was missing out on *Corporate America*, so I decided to be a Corporate Girl. You know, the world will respect me more when I'm strutting into an office, looking the part, and in my *Corporate Role*. So, it hit me to go back to school and become a Certified Biller & Coder for medical facilities. Within a month, I had signed up for classes, had my uniforms, and was going back to school in a few weeks. I was excited! John and the girls were looking at me like I had ten heads.

Reflective Moment

I can still remember the looks on my girls' faces and the fear in their eyes. I remember my daughter, Jadé said to me, "Mommy who's gonna get us ready in the mornings and drop us to school now?" I told her don't worry Daddy will do it. That was the only answer I could come up with.

I knew my schedule was going to be a full day but had no clue how it was going to work out. But I was going to get my life *Together*! I needed to leave before the girls left for school, and I wouldn't be home in time to pick them up from school either; I would have a one-hour commute both ways. Our whole living system was about to change. So here we go! John had to rearrange his schedule most days at work so that he could drop the girls off and pick them up. When possible, I would leave my last class a little early so that I could rush home for pickup. When I got in from school, I went straight upstairs to change my clothes because I had a few clients on their way to get their hair done. The girls would change, grab something in the kitchen, and get straight to doing their homework. John would come in straight from work and go to the kitchen to cook dinner.

We were all so stressed, tired, overwhelmed, and *confused*. We did this for a little over a year until I completed the program. The last step was completing my internship, after which I was immediately hired. I did it! I was working as a Biller/Coder for one of the biggest hospitals in the area. I went to work every day looking sharp with my suits on, looking like a boss and stepping high in my high heels. Everyone thought I was hired as a supervisor because of the way I dressed. Not only did I look good, but I was doing *well*! I was given favor through a Senior Director that my mother-in-love knew very well.

Instead of me waiting 90 days to be in the union, I was enrolled within weeks of working there. One day I came home from work at around 6:30 p.m., and I had four ladies waiting outside my home to get their hair done. And as usual, I didn't get in the bed until after 2:00 a.m., knowing I had to be up by 5:30 a.m. to get to work on time. When I got upstairs that morning, I sat on the edge of the bed and *CRIED*! John says to me, "What's wrong now?" I looked at him with tears in my eyes and said, "*I AM SO UNHAPPY.*" It was then I realized that I had made a *colossal mistake*. I went on like that for another two months. For a total of four months, I cried while driving to work, sitting at my desk, and on my lunch breaks. One day John decided to surprise me at an Italian restaurant where I ate lunch almost every day. He walked in and tapped me on my shoulder. I looked up at him with a face full of tears. He sat down with me and said, "That's it! You're coming home!" I was *SO RELIEVED*! He told me the exact thing I was afraid to tell him! I called out sick for the rest of the week. On the next Monday morning, I went into my supervisor's office and told her I wouldn't be back. She was shocked! She asked me what was wrong. She told me I was doing so well and was up for a pay raise in a few more weeks. I looked her right in her eyes and told her, "*I Don't Belong Here*." She wanted to give me a few days to think about it, but I told her *absolutely not*.

I left her office, went straight to my desk, packed everything up, and was out the door and in my car. Yup! *And, I Cried Tears of Joy Driving Back Home*. When the girls came in from school, we sat them down for our family meeting, and I told them, "I Quit!" They jumped up out their seats dancing, clapping hugging me, and they were even emotional. Jadé looked at me and said, "Mommy, I don't know what you were going through, but *PLEASE*, don't ever do that again." We were all relieved, and immediately my house was back flowing with *Peace* and *Order*.

That experience is just one example of many "*Soul Tantrums*," I've experienced. When your soul is in a state of confusion, everything in your life can look scrambled, confusing, and even pointless. I never needed to change my position from working inside the home to working outside the home. *I Only Needed To Change The Position Of My Soul!*

My soul was in turmoil because it needed to be fed from suffering from malnourishment for 30 years. Listen, your soul is like a child; it is vulnerable, looking for guidance and direction. Even though it doesn't always like it, it wants and needs it.

> **'Eboni' Wisdom**
> You can physically age, but if you are not specifically working on your soul, you will age, but *never* mature.

My soul was searching for *purpose*, which could only be defined by my *Spirit Man*. Purpose isn't defined by what you do. It can only be identified through the revelation of *who God* created you to be. Knowing your purpose is the beginning of having a *Prosperous Soul*.

> **'Eboni' Wisdom**
> A prosperous soul is a maturing soul. You can be *Rich* and *Immature*, but you *Cannot* be *Prosperous* without having a *Mature Soul* that is not stuck in its dysfunctions, but a soul that has been fed, and has done the work to be transformed.

Prosperity comes from within; it produces and is then displayed outwardly. We can see in scripture that a prosperous soul is a requirement of prosperity.

> "Beloved, I pray that you may prosper in all things
> and be in health, just as your soul prospers."
> — III John 1:2 NKJV

Listen, your soul is made from the history of your experiences, where you were raised, how, and by whom. It's also made up of what you saw, were told, the good times, bad times, confusing times, and how you have interpreted *all* of that. Your soul is the part of you that has its own opinions. It is only interested in what you like, how you feel, what you think about everyone and everything, and the decisions you want to make that will best suit *you*. It does not have the ability of its own to think beyond what it already knows. The only language your soul comprehends is *I* and *Me*! Your soul is the part of you that believes that everything you do and say is ok. It will tell you absolutely without a doubt that your *"shenanigans"* are validated. However, when we must deal with the repercussions of our actions, the same *soul* will try to convince you that you *Do Not Deserve* to be in the position you've found yourself in. I know! The soul is out of control! So, even though our soul naturally wants to do its own thing, our soul is really searching for structure, peace, hope, joy, forgiveness, how to love unconditionally, guidance, purpose, clarity, direction, and all of the nutrients it needs to mature and be prosperous. To find answers, your soul will formulate questions within you that only your *Spirit Man*, through *Salvation*, can answer. This revelation is what brings us to our first and necessary wall.

WALL #1 – SALVATION

I love talking about *Salvation* in its simplest form. I am not a Preacher or Theologian, neither do I consider myself a Bible Scholar. But I am a Christian, and I know when I decided to make Jesus Lord over my life, I needed to understand the gift of salvation in its most simplistic form. We cannot receive it if we don't understand it, so, here it is!

Salvation is *Redemption* for *all* humanity. It is the result of the *Ultimate Sacrifice* that saves us from the destruction of sin that results in eternal death. And through Jesus' death and resurrection, God gave us the gift of eternal life after this life. The peace, joy, prosperity, and wholeness that God promised we could have so we may *enjoy* life while here on earth.

I always like to use this example for those of us who have experienced going to the clubs. You know that most clubs have a VIP section. When you get to the door, depending on what time you arrive, most likely, you will stand in line. Now the super long line is for the regular people who are okay with simply being in the club. They don't care about any special treatments, being served, having comfortable lounge chairs, standing out from the crowd; they don't want anything extra. Let them in the club so they can dance and do their regular thing. Come on, you remember! However, the shorter line moves a lot faster. They have more courteous staff that will escort you to the VIP section. You may have some refreshments served to you, including your drink of choice. You'll get special attention. People notice you because your section is usually *High-lighted*, and it includes all the things that the regular people *do not* care about, and more.

Well, *Salvation* is like living life in the *VIP Section!* When you get saved, it should not only be because you don't want to die and go to hell with all the regular people who don't care about life. You should want salvation so that your life can be *High-lighted*, and you can *make an unforgettable mark on this world.* Salvation separates you from the people who are ok with living an ordinary life, who don't believe it's possible to live better, do better, have better, or experience better. What I love about salvation is that it comes with a book load of *benefits* that are available just for you! And guess what, these benefits are *guaranteed* to work! *You Can't Beat That!* The world says that nothing in life is guaranteed, but that's only for people who don't receive salvation. For the *VIP members* who have accepted salvation, they live a life *full* of guarantees.

'Eboni' Wisdom
Receiving *Salvation* is only the beginning of **Christianity**. Your salvation should include a commitment to live a Christ-like lifestyle, so that you can enjoy *all* the benefits that salvation has to offer.

Often when we hear Christians talk about salvation, their focus is mostly on where you will spend eternity. Don't get me wrong this is a very important part of salvation, but I've encountered many people who have told me that they don't even believe that there is life after death. My response to them is always, "Okay, so you don't believe in Heaven or Hell? That's fine, but what happens if after you die, you see that there really is a Heaven and a Hell? Now you're in a pickle!" Think of it like this; driving a car without car insurance is being reckless and could cost you your life. So is dying without salvation; it's *reckless* and will cost you *Eternal Life*. In addition to where you will spend eternity, salvation gives you access to an extraordinary way of living life here on earth that broadens your horizon and opens your soul up to living a lifestyle with endless possibilities. You must know that salvation does not end at saving you from your sins through repentance. It goes even deeper than that by saving you from being controlled by your *Soul*. You can have a beautiful soul when it's aligned with your *spirit*, through *salvation*. Listen, your soul *needs* guidance from your spirit man, and for your spirit man to have access to the ultimate Guidance Counselor, JESUS CHRIST, you must receive salvation.

I will let you in on a secret. I received salvation at a young age. I believe I was between the ages of 10-12. I understood salvation, but I didn't get the revelation of the benefits that it provided for my life here on earth. I struggled with aligning my life with God's principles for many years before I got the revelation that my salvation was also for my soul. It was then I knew that I needed to transform my soul by deprogramming my thinking and submitting my mind to the thoughts of Christ. Receiving Jesus Christ as your personal savior is easy. Actually, you can do it right now. Romans 10:9 says, "Because if you acknowledge and confess with our mouth that Jesus is Lord (recognizing His power, authority, and majesty as God), and believe in your heart that God raised Him from the dead, you will be saved." Yup! It's just that simple. Recite this scripture, receive Him into your heart, ask for forgiveness of your sins, tell God to come into your life, and begin to read His Word to align your life with His principles daily.

WALL #2 – RENEWING YOUR MIND

We are talking about the four walls of the soul. Have you noticed that I haven't mentioned *Church* yet as we move on to *renewing your mind*? Unfortunately, I have found when you bundle salvation with the church, a lot of people become distracted with their preconceived thoughts and ideas about church. Those thoughts and ideas become more important than the *significance* of having a relationship with Jesus Christ. I totally understand. Don't get me wrong, I was born and raised in the church. As an adult, my family and I are members of a church, where my husband and I actively serve. With that said, I've experienced the tremendous benefits of attending church, but I have also experienced "church hurt" and many moments of being completely turned off while attending.

For me, my reasons for attending church have *nothing* to do with people, but *everything* to do with my relationship with Christ. I have decided that I will *never* let anyone or anything stop me from assembling with other believers. Moreover, the scripture encourages us to do just that.

> "Let us seize and hold tightly the confession of our hope without wavering, for He who promised is reliable and trustworthy and faithful [to His word]; and let us consider [thoughtfully] how we may encourage one another to love and to do good deeds, not forsaking our meeting together [as believers for worship and instruction], as is the habit of some, but encouraging one another; and all the more [faithfully] as you see the day [of Christ's return] approaching."
> – Hebrews 10:23-25 AMP

Considering this, if you never want to step foot inside a church for the rest of your life, that is totally up to you. However, *DO NOT* let your decision not to attend stop you from building a relationship with Jesus Christ. I have learned through my relationship with God that there is a church home for everyone. We must allow Him to guide us to where we need to be. Now, let's get into renewing your mind.

If you don't remember anything else from this book, please remember that EB said, "If you can change your *mind*, you can change your *life*." You may have heard this somewhere before, but I need you to take these words *literally,* especially when it comes to the matters of your soul. The only thing that can change the dysfunctions in your soul is intentionally renewing your mind. So how do we begin to renew our minds? Well, the steps are quite simple. In the process of renewing my mind, I initially struggled with the *'consistency'* that's required. However, the more you are in the habit of renewing your mind, I've found it to become *"1st Nature."* So, prayerfully you have already completed step one, which is salvation.

Now, after you have received salvation, you should begin to take the principles of God, read them, write them, speak them, and meditate on them *daily*. For example, the first thing my soul longed for was validation because of the absence of my dad. Once realized, I would look up scriptures that would help validate me. One of my favorites is found in Psalms 139:13-18 AMP. Here is another scripture to get you started. "What then shall we say to all these things? If God is for us, who can be (successful) against us?" (Roman 8:31).

So, I take scripture like the above, using the steps I mentioned, and think about it at least one time within every hour of the day. I wrote scriptures on index cards and carried them daily as a reminder to take the word with me wherever I go. I found quiet time either early in the morning or late in the evenings before bed to reread the scripture to myself, and out loud so I can hear it, works best. Then I sit quietly and think about what I had read. I did one scripture a week but sometimes stayed on certain scriptures longer, until I believed and received what it was saying to me. This was my regimen for a while. My next area for me to tackle was fear, so I followed these same steps and used this scripture below.

"For God did not give us a spirit of timidity or cowardice or fear, but [He has given us a spirit] of power and of love and of sound judgment and personal discipline [abilities that result in a calm, well-balanced mind and self-control]."
− 2 Timothy 1:7 AMP

Exercising conscious thinking leads to intentionally building up your soul. What's great about this practice is the more I transformed my thinking and meditated on the word of God, the more I received clarity in my thoughts and began to receive answers or resolve to the issues and questions that created confusion in my mind. I began to have a settling in my soul and spirit as they began to fuse and become one. I like to call this a *"Soul Fusion."* I like to compare this *Soul Fusion* to your *Soul* and *Spirit* working together, just like a knife and fork cutting through a nice thick steak. The soul controls your body, and it is like the fork picking up food to put it in your mouth in an effort for your body to digest. However, it needs the knife (the spirit) because it cuts, separates, divides, and takes away the unnecessary pieces that *You* don't like. Also, the knife removes the pieces you like, but are not good for you, and creates smaller portions to help you control how much you put in your mouth, so you don't choke and kill yourself. Most importantly, it can *Destroy*.

The more I participated in this *Soul Fusion*, I began seeing my behavior change. My usual way of responding to situations was replaced with a more mature response. I was learning how to be disciplined and exercise self-control, especially in difficult situations. I noticed I was building my character and integrity by focusing on my soul. I was finally in control of my thoughts by thinking *"on purpose"* by taking negative and self-centered thinking and replacing those thoughts with the word of God. You may ask if I was tempted at any time during this process to resort back to my old way of thinking? Of Course! But every time temptation came, I would grab a scripture and speak it out my mouth and say to myself, "No, that's not how I think, *My Thoughts Are Aligned With The Word of God."*

> **'Eboni' Wisdom**
> The world insinuates that your brain is a part
> of your body that you cannot control.

I'm not a doctor, and by no means am I negating there are medical issues that can affect our brains. However, even if you need medication for assistance, you still have the authority over your thoughts. When God created you, *He* gave you authority over all things, and that included your brain. Having a mind of Christ is one of your God-given rights as a believer. For those of us who have received *salvation* (the VIP members), we received *Holy Spirit,* and *He* has the *Power* to control our brains. I have witnessed many people I know who have committed to renewing their minds. And, as a result, they have completely come off their medication. *Renewing your Mind* is *Guaranteed* to work! Renewing my mind has changed my thinking forever. I have committed to making it a vital part of my lifestyle. I pray you too will join me and commit to *Renewing Your Mind Daily*!

"And do not be conformed to this world [any longer with its superficial values and customs], but be transformed and progressively changed [as you mature spiritually] by the renewing of your mind [focusing on godly values and ethical attitudes], so that you may prove [for yourselves] what the will of God is, that which is good and acceptable and perfect [in His plan and purpose for you]."
— Romans 12:2 AMP

WALL #3 – A PROGRESSIVE LIFESTYLE

After you have received *salvation*, and have committed to *renewing* your mind daily, begin taking a closer look at your lifestyle. I meet a lot of Christians who think that their daily regimens will automatically change. I wish it were that easy! During the process of doing my own *self-work*, I have learned that thinking on purpose is just as significant as *Living On Purpose*. Progress does not come without *effort*. To live a '*Progressive Lifestyle*,' we must make a conscious decision to stop doing things that impede our progress. Taking time to reevaluate your lifestyle periodically helps you become more aware of the progress you're currently making and allows you to adjust what's necessary to move forward. For example, most successful corporations have monthly or weekly meetings with their staff members to reevaluate how the company is functioning, their progress made, and to come up with new strategies that will make the company develop further. You also must sit down with your supervisor, manager, Vice President, or President, to receive a personal evaluation of your individual progress and your improvements needed to move forward. Because of this consistent checking in process, these corporations are highly competitive and do exceptionally well. Why? Because they are committed to making sure they are continually making *Progress*. Now, imagine if we all as individuals did that in our personal lives? How much further along would we be? Living a *'Progressive Lifestyle'* consists of us making those same efforts. So how do we put this into action?

As you can tell, I like to come up with my own names and phrases for just about everything. It's my way of making things more personal so that I can internalize it better.

So, I like to say that a *'Progressive Lifestyle'* requires *"Do Better Living."* And this term keeps it simple for me. You may be thinking, what is that? *Do Better Living* is when you wake up in the morning and make a conscious decision that you're going to do something better than how you did it yesterday. It may sound juvenile to you, but this principle has changed my *entire* life.

I am doing things I have never imagined doing just by concentrating on doing something better every day.

Reflective Moment
I once had what people might consider a bad attitude.

Maybe you can identify with me. People would say that my attitude was a bit standoffish, uninviting, stuck up, and have called me unapproachable. Now I am not controlled by people's opinions, however, when the people who I value, and are close to, started saying the same thing, I began to *evaluate* myself and see what adjustments I needed to make.

'Eboni' Wisdom
When you select people to be your "Best Friends" or connect with people that you say you love, value, and can confide in, you should also trust when they tell you things about yourself you may not like to hear. Know it is coming from a place of love, and a desire to want to see you *Be Better*.

I was unconsciously unaware, but after taking a close look, I realized I was using my lousy attitude as a defense mechanism to protect myself from being hurt by people. It was a bad habit that I needed to break. Though I had done the work of forgiving people that hurt me in the past and was renewing my mind to move forward, I had not made an intentional effort to change the *behavior* which came along with that hurt. Behaviors can be very addictive. If we're not careful, we can become blinded by them, and they become unconscious participants. I even noticed if John and I were out running errands or in the supermarket, people would walk past me, walk right up to him and start talking to him. People would ask his opinion, or even his help in deciding about what they were purchasing, while I am standing right there. He is still often told by total strangers how approachable he is; they can just look and feel free to speak to him. These episodes further confirmed this was something I needed to change, not for people but *Me*, so it wouldn't be a hindrance and keep me from making the progress I wanted.

You already know what I did first. I prayed and asked God to help me with my attitude. Then I grabbed a scripture that would change my thinking and support me in having a pleasant demeanor. Finally, I would wake up every morning and say to myself, "Self, today we are going to make a conscious, consistent choice to have a positive attitude all day." It didn't matter whether I liked everything that transpired throughout my day or not; my *attitude* was going to remain *positive*.

Now, initially, there were days where I didn't always get this right. Some days I would start out doing great, and then someone would say something, or a situation would happen, and my attitude was shot for the rest of the day. But I did not give up! I would get right back up the next day and commit to myself that today I am going to 'Do Better' than I did yesterday.

'Eboni' Wisdom

The first word in this phrase is 'Do,' means to actively participate. And, this is the only way we will be able to live a *Progressive Lifestyle*. We can't just limit ourselves to transforming inwardly, we must also commit to changing our behaviors so there can be an outward show that reaches the people we encounter.

"But prove yourselves doers of the word [actively and continually obeying God's precepts], and not merely listeners [who hear the word but fail to internalize its meaning], deluding yourselves [by unsound reasoning contrary to the truth]."

– James 1:22 AMP

As the days turned into weeks, months, and years, my attitude was changing. And today, it is transformed. I remember the first time John and I were out, and a stranger walked over to me and said, "I was searching for someone I could ask this question, and I looked over at you, your *aura* was so pleasant. I knew I could walk over and talk to you." Well, I felt like I was on that television show, "The Price is Right!" I heard that winning music playing and the bells were ringing in my head! I wanted to take off running through the store, screaming, "*I WON, I WON!*"

Now, people talk to me when we are out more than they talk to John. He is so tickled by this and always says, "Babe, remember when people wouldn't talk to you? Now you can't stop them from running up on you. You Go Girl!"

Reflective Moment

I thank God for John being the person who challenges me and always makes sure I am making progress. It's very important you surround yourself with people who are also living a *Progressive Lifestyle*. Their support helps you to stay focused and receive support in challenging times because they too understand.

People who know me now, especially my mentees, are shocked when they hear my story. They share how they can't imagine me having a bad attitude. Their reaction is always "No EB, Not You!" This is just one of many examples, but I declare that *"Do Better Living,"* *Really* works.

If you can take this principle and work it in every area of your life, you will begin to see the progress you're making is *Mind Blowing*. You will also accomplish your short and long-term goals. What I love about a *Progressive Lifestyle* is it removes all the limits we place on ourselves. Progress never runs out! You can always find ways to think, live, and be better. Your progress is governed by you and the choice to do better.

Living a *Progressive Lifestyle* requires you to be accountable to God and yourself. Sometimes we are more committed to being accountable to others than we are to God. When I committed to God that I would live a *Progressive Lifestyle*, it was great. Then when I added myself to this commitment, I felt a sense of self-worth. My character and integrity were strengthened. I began to love myself more because I was proud of whom I was becoming. My self-esteem is continuously renewed by living a *Progressive Lifestyle*. Every day, we *must* make sure we are progressing in some way, shape, or form. Ultimately it is you who should want to live a life that is pleasing to God. Listen, *God Loves Progress!* I know you are shocked, but nobody wants you to progress more than *He* does. The whole reason God sent His Son to die for us is because He wanted us to *Do Better*. Now we have no excuse! We can ask for forgiveness for our sins, receive *Grace and Mercy*, and work at it again. Wanting to please God with your life is the root of *Progressive Living*. When you make this your focus, you will see that living a *Progressive Lifestyle* is inevitable.

> "Meditate on these things; give yourself entirely to them, that your progress may be evident to all."
> – 1 Timothy 4:15 NKJV

WALL #4 – SACRIFICE TO SERVE

Last but certainly not least, we have our final *Soul Strengthening* wall. I believe that *Sacrifice* is one of the many precious principles God desires for us to be an active participant. When you position your heart for people, the action prepares and causes you to receive all that God has for you. I always say that building a relationship with God is like building a relationship when you're dating. You spend a lot of time together, resulting in becoming like each other in several areas. So, it's the same when you spend more time in the presence of God and building a relationship with Him. You start to want what He wants, what He likes, and desires. You hate what He hates and love people as He does. Sacrifice is a part of who Jesus is. He was a prime example of this while He was here on earth. He showed us that we should sincerely and wholeheartedly care for people. His heart was always in a position to *Sacrifice* for others. He did not just view us as people, but He saw us as *Souls* that needed to be saved, healed, delivered, and set free.

Sacrifice is one of those principles that require a culmination of principles working together in sync for you to operate within successfully. For instance, if you have not worked the principle of forgiveness, then it will be hard for you to sacrifice successfully. If you are a prideful person, and you are not operating in principles like peace, patience, submission, or gratitude, you will struggle with the principle of *Sacrifice*. A lot of people negatively look at the word *Sacrifice*. The world tends to tell us that when you sacrifice, you are setting yourself back, you're missing out, neglecting yourself, and putting yourself at risk to go without, indefinitely. This view is way out of balance and, in my opinion, simply not true. I don't believe that this is the kind of sacrifice that God requires of us. God requires us to have a heart for people to where we don't mind going out our way, rearranging our schedules, or even being inconvenienced, to meet someone else's needs. However, this can only happen if you genuinely have a heart for and desire to see people win. Remember, our primary purpose is to be God's representatives in the earth, which means we must be His hands, feet, mouth, and have His heart. Well, do we think we can do all of this for God, and not have our plans occasionally interrupted?

I remember in one of our monthly mentoring meetings, God gave me a question to ask the group. "Can you please excuse this interruption?" It was a revelation for them and me. So many times, we get so upset, annoyed, and sometimes angry because someone or something interrupted our plans for the day. So, if people cannot interrupt you, then *Holy Spirit* definitely cannot interrupt you. Have you ever been in a conversation and a person keeps interrupting you while you are speaking? Mannnn, you almost want to fight them, and you are thinking, *"That is So Rude."* Well, we have conditioned ourselves in thinking that *all* interruptions are rude. However, some interruptions are *Necessary*. For example: If crossing the street and you have the right of way, and someone unexpectedly runs up to you and grabs you out from being run over by a reckless driver, are you upset with them because they interrupted your plans of walking across the street? NO!! Because they just saved your life, that interruption was *necessary*, and now that it is safe for you to cross the street. Guess what? This time you are paying more attention. You are wiser now because of the incident you just experienced.

This is the same way I want you to look at the *Sacrifice to Serve*. Anytime *Holy Spirit* lays it on your heart to sacrifice your plans, schedule, daily regimen, and be inconvenienced so you can meet someone else's needs, it is because He wants to have an impact on both of your lives. Sacrificing to serve others has saved my life. I have watched people die spiritually and physically from being consumed with selfishness. All they think about is themselves, and everything revolves around them. They only can hang around people that tell them how wonderful they are and people who can benefit them. These people are often *empty* on the inside; no matter what they do for themselves, they are never satisfied. Some of them even think the more things they buy for themselves, the happier they will be, but it never works. This selfish lifestyle can lead to depression because of the unbearable loneliness and lack of purpose they feel internally. Sadly, many have taken their own lives because *Selfishness Will Never Satisfy You*.

Whenever I go out my way to be a blessing to someone else, not only were they blessed, but I walk away from that experience *changed* for the better. I always receive revelation, a different perspective, and am amazed at how powerful God's principles are. My level of *Gratitude* is increased more and more. Listen, when you understand the benefits of *sacrifice,* you will look for opportunities to serve others. It wasn't until I learned how to sacrifice that I started to experience not only the blessings of God in my life but His unimaginable Favor on my life. Most importantly, the *joy* I have experienced in seeing other people benefit, and advance because of my sacrifices, has added to the satisfaction of knowing I am walking in my purpose.

> ### Reflective Moment
> When I reflect on the many days I felt empty, it was because
> I wasn't fulfilling my purpose. Now, fast forward, I am now literally
> impacting lives and assisting God in drawing people to Him. I am now
> complete and whole.

I remember a recent health issue that my doctors presented to me. Ladies, you know how we go for our yearly mammograms, just as the gentleman must go for prostate checkups, etc. Usually, you are at least 40 when required to have these exams done unless otherwise recommended. Well, I have a nodule in my breasts. Doctors have been monitoring for 14 years. Don't try it! I'm only 43. One time, they suspected this nodule had grown and wanted to do a biopsy to test it. Well, you know initially my flesh wants to have me upset, but thank God for my husband, daughters, Pastor, and Pastor's wife. I was able to bring my thoughts back into alignment with the promises of God. I am *Eternally Grateful* for all of them! I am *Blessed* and *Honored* to have them in my life.

So, the day I had my biopsy was the same day, John and I were scheduled to have a mentoring session with the young ladies at a shelter. Initially, it was no big deal to me because I'm thinking a biopsy cannot be that painful. Well, call me a big baby because I surely cried the entire time I was on that table. I was mentally and emotionally drained. My breast was *very* sore, aching, and throbbing. I left the doctor's office with the bandages and an ice pack in my bra. The nurse suggested I go straight home, with very little activity because they wanted to keep the bleeding down to a minimum. When I got in the car John asked me, do you still want to go to the shelter? Everything in me wanted to say *No*. However, I began to think about the young homeless moms who were looking forward to seeing us. They were waiting for us to sit with them and pour into their spirits. I started to think about how this could be the day we saved them from making a bad choice they could regret for the rest of their lives. Today could be the day where one word said to them would give them that "AHH HAHH" moment to transform their thinking. I couldn't help thinking about how *Grateful* they are when we come, and how they tell us about the *Peace* they feel even after we leave. Most importantly, what we do for them not only helps them but helps their children.

Yes, I was extremely uncomfortable; I wanted to go home and crawl up in my bed and be pampered by my darling husband that evening, with my mind on my biopsy results. But I remembered an old saying of my grandmother, "What you make happen for others God will make happen for you." So, I'm saying to myself if I *Sacrifice to Serve* these young mothers, by assisting them in their healing process, then God *Promised* He *Will* do the same for me. Well, I grabbed me a healing scripture, and I made the sacrifice to go to the shelter. I am so glad we went! The meeting was fantastic! The young ladies kept saying how much they are learning and growing in forgiveness and mending their relationships with family members by attending our meetings. They were more touched when John shared with them what I had been through a few hours earlier. We stressed to them the importance of going out their way to bless others even in times where it's a sacrifice for them. I am *Blessed* to say I received my results three days later and, I am cancer *FREE*! Just as much as this *Sacrifice* benefitted the young moms, it was a huge benefit to me. I learned so many things from that moment. Most importantly, I learned that when I keep my mind on the things of God and make what *HE* wants me to do, my focus, worry, and fear *Could Not Overtake Me*.

Wherever you find yourself in life today, know you can always be a blessing to someone else. Your sacrifice might be giving someone an encouraging word even when you don't feel encouraged yourself. Or maybe it's you giving up your seat to an older person on the train, although you are exhausted and want to sit down. There are many ways to *Sacrifice to Serve*. So, don't minimize your sacrifice, for God does not measure by how big or small. He measures those moments by our *Hearts* and our willingness to serve. Just like anything else we do, we must have balance in *All Things*. Always pray for God's wisdom, and I promise you, Holy Spirit will lead you and guide you in your *Sacrifices*.

Eboni Wisdom

God *Never* expects us to abuse ourselves in any area of our lives, He wants us to always maintain a *Heart To Serve*.

"But do not forget to do good and to share,
for with such sacrifices, God is well pleased."
– Hebrews 13:16 NKJV

This principle is now part of my lifestyle, and I pray you are encouraged to make it part of yours. *Trust God, Sacrifice to Serve and You Will Not Regret It!*

CHAPTER IV –
BEHIND THE 4 WALLS OF LIFE

The word 'life' is a small four-letter word with a *HUGE* meaning. Talking about life, in general, can become intense, overwhelming, and bring up a lot of good and bad emotions. When discussing life with my mentees, I try to make it as least stressful as possible. My motto continues to be "Keep it simple." So, I came up with four walls that will help support you in this journey called life. When you apply these four simple words and use them as principles to live by, your life and those around you will be enhanced. The four words are *Learn*, *Influence*, *Fruit*, and *Expectation*. Yes, it's easy to remember, because it is an acronym for the word *LIFE*. There are many more principles I could add to this chapter, but I believe that these four are a great place to start. So, let's get into it!

WALL #1 – LIVING A LEARNING LIFE

We have been learning since the day we were born. Doctors say we were learning while we were still in our mother's womb. As we have now become adults, it is important to always position ourselves to *Learn*. Some people only set themselves to learn if they are in some type of school setting that has been set up for them to receive a certificate, license, degree, etc. When in these types of environments, people are completely open to learning whatever they need to complete their selected course. Well, *Life* is a course that we all need to complete, and to do so *successfully*, we must be open to learning from it. *Everyday* living provides a learning experience, even if it's something you may consider minut. When I first received the revelation years ago, I felt like it was impossible to learn something every day. In my ignorance, I didn't realize that my life had become mundane for reasons such as this, not making a conscious effort to *Learn*. We can remain stagnant and live very dull lives just because we don't choose to learn on purpose. Do you know what this world would be like if people didn't learn? Eventually, we would die due to the lack thereof. Learning is imperative and necessary for life and growth.

Learning consists of you *Collecting and Processing* information about people, places, things, and yourself. It's one thing to collect information, which is the easy part, but that information is not beneficial to *You* unless you take the time to process it for personal application. I've learned that there is a lesson in *Everything*. So, I began to challenge myself, and I continue to this day. At the end of *every day,* I ask myself, 'EB, what did you learn today?' I made up in my mind to no longer live life without learning. As you have probably heard many times before, *Knowledge Is Power*. It's so true! The more you know, the more you grow! There are so many things we can learn from if willing. You can look back at your personal life experiences and learn today from something you experienced years ago.

I recall my experience of being a teenage mom. I was encouraging another teen mom by sharing my story of becoming pregnant at 19. When I got home, I sat down and continued thinking about that journey. I thought to myself, 'Wow, you learned a lot about yourself during that time.' I began to connect some of the strengths I have today with the weaknesses I felt back then. Holy Spirit began to show me how much I grew and matured during that time. I remember when I first found out I was pregnant; my body was feeling a bit weird for about four months prior to me finding out. I still had a menstrual cycle until the 4th month of my pregnancy. They were becoming lighter and lighter, but hey, I didn't overthink why. And *I definitely* didn't want to think I was pregnant. I was becoming very nauseous, felt sleepy often, and my energy was lowering. I remember going on a family vacation to Florida. Lord! I was so sick, it was so hot there, and I was exhausted even when I just woke up. I wasn't feeling good *at all*. One day we went to the amusement park, and I remember standing on line to get on a rollercoaster. I felt so weak standing in the sun, and I thought I was going to faint. Finally, I get on the ride, and *JESUS HELP ME*! When I got off the ride, I was a mess! It took everything in me not to throw up. I felt dizzy and weak, and I just wanted to lie down. I had been communicating with John while I was there, so he was aware of how bad I had been feeling. After a week, my family and I returned home, and I was relieved to be back in my room and my bed. Now listen to this!

One day after we returned from our trip, John called me and said, "Hey," I said, "Hey, what's up!" He replied, "Well, I'm just calling you to tell you that you are *Pregnant*." *RIGHT*!! I said, "*HUH*?" He's said, "Yeah, I didn't know how to tell you. Since you've been feeling so bad lately, I didn't want you to think something was wrong with you; you're just pregnant." 'Ohhhhh JUST Pregnant,' I thought to myself. I burst out into a laugh! I said, "*BOY, YOU ARE CRAZY*!" Well, later in the day, he comes to pick me up to go hang out, and after a long conversation, we decide to pick up a pregnancy test. YUPP!! Your girl was pregnant.

I remember the many different emotions I felt like *Acceptance, Alone, Angry,* and *Confused. I was Disappointed but, Elated, Excited, but then felt like I Failed. I became Fearful but Happy, Hopeful yet Hopeless. I felt Joy, Love, Rejection, and was Terrified all at the same time.* Talk about an *Emotional Overload*! I'm sure many of you can relate to being in a position where you have experienced many different emotions, seemingly at the same time. These feelings stayed with me throughout my entire pregnancy, which caused me to be *Very Emotional*. I used to sit in my room in one thought excited about my baby, wondering what she looked like. I anticipated holding her and gazing into her beautiful eyes, combing her hair, dressing her up, talking, and playing with her. However, in the very next thought, I was scared out of my mind, trying to figure out if I could stay focused enough to finish hair school to get my license and provide for my daughter. I was disappointed in myself for getting pregnant at 19, and I felt uncertain about John's intent to stick around and help me. I was overwhelmed with wondering if he would leave me and my baby like my father left me. I was unsure about everything, myself, my relationship, my career, *my Life*. I heard so many stories about what women couldn't do or become because they got pregnant at a young age. I didn't have a plan and had no clue how to make one.

Furthermore, should my plans include John, or should they be about my baby and me? That was some of my inner turmoil. On top of that, when I added in what people would *Say and Think*, I would breakdown.

'Eboni' Wisdom

To every teenage mom who will read this book:
Know that *God Still Has A Plan For You*. You may feel like you can't make it, perhaps confused about how to move forward, or even feel like giving up. *Don't Give Up*! Everything you need to be a *successful woman*, and an *amazing mother*, has already been placed inside you by God. It is your job to mature, develop, and grow up in Him. Take each principle mentioned, and work on them. Doing so, will be one of the best investments you've made in yourself. Before you know it, and with the help of Holy Spirit, you will be proud of yourself, and the person you are *becoming*.

Although this time was difficult, *I Learned A Lot*. I continue to learn from my experience. I also learned I could do anything I put my mind to. I graduated, took my state board test while I was nine months pregnant, and received my license in the mail shortly after Jadé was born. I learned what it meant to truly "require God as my *Essential Source*." I went to God about everything. I asked Him to help me walk to the train station in the wintertime so I wouldn't fall while pregnant, walking through the snow and on ice. I asked Him to keep Jadé and I safe as we rode on the "A-Train" late hours in the night.

I had to stay late to take clients in the evenings to make enough money to buy pampers, clothes, milk, etc. I asked God to always have a nice man at the train steps who would help me carry Jadé's stroller up two long flights of steps. Yes, no matter what time it was, a nice gentleman was *Always* there. I even asked Him to comfort my heart so that I could stay focused on my goals while being the best mom possible. I learned what it felt like to love someone more than I loved myself. I learned how to sacrifice what I wanted to do, for what *I needed* to do because my baby girl was more important to me than *My* wants. I learned what *Love* truly is, because I had this baby that I wanted to protect, support, nurture, be attentive to, and invest my time in. I wanted to give her the absolute best version of me so that she could be great. I learned *Agape (Unconditional) Love*, which gave me a clear revelation of how *God Loves Me*. Nothing that this baby could *EVER* do will stop me from loving her with *All* my heart. I learned to have *Courage*, even though at times, I was terrified of how different my new life would be. However, with fear, I kept reaching for my goals and was determined that one day I would be the mother that Jadé would be proud of.

Ultimately, I learned how to *Worship God*, right in my room, just me, Jadé, and God. I knew that God loved me unconditionally, even when I was feeling bad about becoming a teen mother, unprepared, and not married; I could feel His love for me through my worship to Him. He forgave me and helped me get through every situation, and 23 years later, I am *Grateful For It All*! Today! Jade' is a beautiful, smart, strong, vivacious, focused, mature, ambitious, loving, courageous, innovative, creative, stunning, caring, nurturing, giving, determined, confident (ok I will stop) young lady. She is 23 with a master's degree, has maintained honors status from the age of two when she started school. And guess what y'all *SHE IS STILL A VIRGIN*!

If you had asked me 23 years ago if I saw myself here, I would tell you *Yes*! Why? Because I made a conscious decision to seek God in every area of my life. Likewise, from the day I became a mother, I've asked Holy Spirit to help me make the right decisions to lead Jadé to her purpose so that she can be *All* that God predestined for her to be. I continue to do the same with all three of my girls.

Let every day be a day that you learn on purpose and from the people around you, whether young or old. Learn from what people say and *don't* say. Learn from the way people treat you and how you treat them. Learn from your family members, friends, total strangers, and your enemies. I always say, "*Everyone is a Teacher*." Learn from what is around you. For instance, we use these electronic devices for many purposes, why not use them to research valuable information that will enhance and help us to grow. Learn from the various places you visit or search out information on areas you would like to visit in the future. *Exposure is Everything*! Learn from your past experiences, ask Holy Spirit to reveal to you the lessons in each of them. Apply every lesson to your life so that you can continue to develop the *Greatness* within you. Never Stop Learning!

In a nutshell, be a student *Always*, humble yourself to hear, remain *Flexible* (it makes it easier to learn), remember *Exposure* (will teach you your options), and, most importantly, *Trust God!* With Him on your side, you will never "win or lose," you will only *Win and Learn.*

> "So, here's what I want you to do, God helping you: Take your everyday, ordinary life—your sleeping, eating, going-to-work, and walking-around life—and place it before God as an offering. Embracing what God does for you is the best thing you can do for Him. Don't become so well-adjusted to your culture that you fit into it without even thinking. Instead, fix your attention on God. You'll be changed from the inside out. Readily recognize what He wants from you, and quickly respond to it. Unlike the culture around you, always dragging you down to its level of immaturity, God brings the best out of you, develops well-formed maturity in you."
> – Romans 12:1-2 MSG

WALL #2 – LIVING A LIFE OF INFLUENCE

If there is one thing that amazes me, it is our ability as humans to *Influence* one another. Influence is a *powerful* thing, and the reason why we must use it positively. I chose to use influence as one of the four walls of life because we must live a lifestyle that influences others and leads them to God.

What a revelation it was for me when I realized that I, Me, little old Eboni, a girl from the "ghetto," could influence others to be *great*, just by me *choosing* and *deciding* to be *Great* myself. It is precisely what God intended for us to do on the earth. This is one of my favorite scriptures speaking about our influence.

"Let me tell you why you are here. You're here to be salt-seasoning that brings out the God-flavors of this earth. If you lose your saltiness, how will people taste godliness? You've lost your usefulness and will end up in the garbage. "Here's another way to put it: You're here to be light, bringing out the God-colors in the world. God is not a secret to be kept. We're going public with this, as public as a city on a hill. If I make you light-bearers, you don't think I'm going to hide you under a bucket, do you? I'm putting you on a light stand. Now that I've put you there on a hilltop, on a light stand—shine! Keep open house; be generous with your lives. By opening to others, you'll prompt people to open up with God, this generous Father in heaven."
– Matthew 5:13-16 MSG

This is how we should use our influence!

In my one-on-one mentoring sessions and at a certain point of our journey of doing

Self-work, I ask my mentees, "Who are *You* influencing?" Why? Because we must fully understand that our lives are not our own. We cannot become satisfied with living a self-centered life that only re-volves around us. It is a trick from the devil to make you miserable and keep you from living a purpose-driven, fulfilled life. Listen, influ-ence not only benefits others, but it also benefits you too. The more we build others, the more we, in turn, build ourselves. I always say, 'water cannot run through a pipe, and the pipe does not get wet,' it is *Impossible*. I believe that we all are assigned to certain people. Along this journey called life, we should ask God to help us to use our influ-ence to fulfill those assignments. Whether it is hands-on influence or you influencing people watching from afar, they both are important and serve a purpose in the lives of others.

When I received the revelation on a personal level of the importance of influence, it caused me to rethink my circle, and the surrounding people I hung out with regularly. You may not believe me, but you can look at the people you surround yourself with and see exactly where your life is headed. The people you listen to, take advice from, look to for instruction, and consider their opinions are a clear picture of what your life will look like in the future. I know you've heard the saying before, "You are what you eat," but I like to say, *"You Are Who You Hang With."* You can learn a lot about a person by just viewing their friends. So, I began to evaluate my circle. I added some people and eliminated others, so I could have people around me that reflect the direction I was trying to go in life.

'Eboni' Wisdom
Evaluating is not a one-time adjustment but something you should do periodically throughout the course of your life.

You might ask, 'Why EB?' I'm glad you asked. As you *Mature and Grow*, your circle *Must Mature and Grow.* The influence they have on you is vital and plays a determining factor in whether you will reach your goals or not. My grandmother used to say, "If you hang around dogs, you can catch fleas." Ha! Whatever is on them will jump on you. Always remember that some friends are for a season, and others are for a lifetime. Ask God for His *Wisdom and Discernment*, and you will know the difference.

I like to use this example. Would you want someone to buy you some beautiful diamond earrings and wrap them in *feces*, put them in a raggedy box and give it to you as a gift? *NO! EXACTLY!* That is how we are when we present ourselves to the world and are surrounded by people who do not reflect who we are. Our life goals are far from God's *Goals and Purpose* placed on the inside of us to share with the world. Well, let me tell you, changing my circle was one of the best things I could have ever done. I noticed that I began to feel more positive.

I was happier and excited about living life. Even the conversation was different, more thought-provoking, and challenged me to want to *be better*. As a married woman, I wanted to make sure our circle had other strong couples that could be a positive influence on our marriage. This is important! John and I went through this process together. We have found that it makes life easier for us when we choose our circle together. And it's an in-depth conversation every time we re-evaluate our circle. We believe that everything has a purpose, including relationships. The influence that comes from your relationships should be *Helpful and not Harmful*. Influence should go both ways within your circle. It is an exchange, and we make sure that we are influencing the people in our circle just as much as they are influencing us.

I've talked about being influenced by people up-close and personally, but I've also been heavily influenced by people I look up to from afar. There are some people who I have never met personally who have affected me to be a better woman, wife, mother, mentor, etc. Women who I have chosen to watch and glean from because their lives provoke me to stay focused and to never give up on my dreams. Both aspects of influence have allowed me to influence others in ways I never thought I could. I use my life experiences to motivate, support, empower, and encourage others. Everything I have experienced, including my challenges are used as opportunities to influence others.

By now, you already have an idea of the challenges I faced in building a relationship with my father. Because I worked hard to get to the place where we were, when he transitioned, I began feeling sad that our relationship was coming to an end. I remembered crying a lot and feeling anxious as his funeral was approaching. At one point,

I remember praying, and I said to God, *"This is SO UNFAIR."* It was then Holy Spirit said to me, "This *relationship* doesn't have to die because your father physically died. The love you experienced in this relationship was based on how you both *Related* to each other, and that has produced something in you that will *never* die." I said, "WOWWWW!" So, that means every time I share our journey with other people, our relationship lives on? Every time I reflect on our unconditional love for one another, our relationship lives on? Most importantly, every time I use my experience to *INFLUENCE* another parent/child relationship, to make them stronger, *our relationship lives on?* At that moment it came to me! I'm going to use our relationship as a testimony of how God can heal your broken heart and mend broken family relationships. My debut announcement to myself and the world was going to be at my father's funeral. As I stood by his casket and shared, I felt the *STRENGTH* from our relationship rising inside of me. I shared how we relied on God throughout our relationship to guide us into how we needed to love on one another. I shared only the *Great* things about him and made it clear to those who were there that his shortcomings were what made our relationship *So Powerful.* I shared the strength that he exhibited even in his weaknesses, and determination he possessed. I also talked about how he sometimes gave up, and the *Faith* he had in God when no one had faith in or believed in Him. It was remarkable. I shared how my father was indeed a worshipper and how his joy was complete in God. I laughed as I shared his comical ways and gestures that got on everyone's nerves at times but made him *Unique.* That day was a day of celebration for me as I presented to family and friends. *A HERO.* An Honorable Man who taught me *More Than He Will Ever Know.* I also presented to them a *relationship* that will *never* die, because if I commit to using our relationship to *Influence Others*, it will always *Live On.*

I pray through my sharing; you have received a full revelation of how powerful *Your Influence* can be. Always remember to be the complete *Strong, Honest, and Unique* version of you. Be willing to use your life experiences to positively influence others. It is what makes your *Influence Great*; it draws others to you and makes them want to know the *GOD* in You. *Influence is Power!*

WALL #3 – LIVING A FRUITFUL LIFE

I chose to make wall #3 in this chapter *Fruit* because I think we don't value this principle enough. We all have a list of *Life Priorities* we've created for ourselves. The list may include your ultimate life goals, career goals, being a role model for your children, a particular lifestyle you ultimately want to live, leaving a legacy for your family and others to appreciate and be proud of, etc. However, when we review our list, how far down on the list is our *Desire to Bear Fruit*?

I know for me personally, initially bearing fruit wasn't on my list of life priorities. In my mind, I was thinking I must get my life together before I can think about being an example or helping anyone else. Don't get me wrong, I agree to a certain extent with this thought, because I know my heart was in the right place as it pertained to being committed to doing my self-work. However, I can wholeheartedly say that concentrating on just yourself for an extended period can do more harm than good. You may ask, "EB, why do you say this?" I'm glad you asked! I say this because we weren't created to be *Self-Centered*. When God created us, He did so in His image, and there is *Nothing* self-centered about God. Just think, God sent His only Son to earth to die for our sins so that we can have *Eternal Life*, and *Enjoy a Purpose Filled, Fruit Filled* life on earth. When God created this world, He created it with *Us* in mind. God strategically created everything on this earth for our specific needs. Even when He made man, He put on the inside of us everything needed and necessary for life, so that we could live a *Fruitful* life. I will go further to say that everything God created, He created to *Bear Fruit*, and likewise, we are created to *Bear Fruit*. What does *Bear Fruit* mean? It means to *Produce* something. Now we know though God created us in His image, we still must make a conscious decision to submit our lives to Him (receive salvation) through Jesus Christ His Son. Salvation allows us to take full advantage of the benefits of living the life God predestined for us to live. *We, as believers, know that God has chosen us to Bear Fruit.*

"You have not chosen Me, but I have chosen you, and I have appointed and placed and purposefully planted you, so that you would go and bear fruit and keep on bearing, and that your fruit will remain and be lasting, so that whatever you ask of the Father in My name [as My representative] He may give to you."
– John 15:16 AMP

So, we are here to be fruitful, produce, create, procreate, reproduce, multiply, and ultimately to be examples, and show *Proof* to the world that *God is Real*, His *Word is True*, and *His Principles Work*. Now, if we have a clear understanding of what it means to *Bear Fruit*, how can this principle not be at the top of our list of "Life Priorities?" When I received this revelation, it added more fuel to *My Purpose!* The more I thought about how important it is for me to live a *Fruitful* lifestyle for God, I became more committed to becoming who He has created me to *Be*. I feel like bearing fruit for God is the *least* I can do for Him; after all He has done and is doing for me. I want God to know that this is not a one-way relationship. I don't ever want Him to feel like I take Him for granted. So, living a *Fruitful* life is my response to God, and my way of telling Him *EVERYTHING* in me says, "*I LOVE YOU,* and *I AM GRATEFUL.*"

Now that we've discussed *Why* we should *Bear Fruit,* let's discuss *How!* As we come to the end of this portion of "Behind These Four Walls," you should have realized one thing about me by now. *I Want You To Win!* I feel like we are often told what we *Should* do, but are not often *Told or Shown, How* to do it. In every chapter, and for every wall (principle), my goal is to give you specific tools you can apply to your life so that you can see the promises of God come to fruition in your life. The principle of *Fruit* is no different. Listen, even God's Word bears fruit! This is the reason He commands us to live by His Word so that we can see with our own eyes and *In* our own lives, what His Word can *Produce.*

'Eboni' Wisdom
God will never ask you to do something that He doesn't do himself. This concept should be a rule of thumb for us as well. You shouldn't require others to do something you're not willing or requiring yourself to do. It shows a lack of character and integrity, and it *Spoils Your Fruit.*

Living a fruitful life is simple. At first, receiving this revelation had me on a "fruit scare."

I put myself under pressure and kept telling myself, "You must bear fruit, come on, where is your fruit?" However, I noticed the first place we should want to see fruit in is our homes. Yes, your fruit-bearing starts with the people you live with. Frankly, home is where fruit-bearing counts. There is nothing better than the people who are with you daily, who see you at your worst and see you at your best, can stand up for you and say that your lifestyle has truly impacted them and changed them for the *Better.* I've found that it also teaches your loved ones how to bear fruit for themselves.

I remember my baby girl Janiya, who we enrolled in kindergarten one year earlier than the recommended age. Her birthday is on

Christmas Eve, so the school said that they could take her at the age of four because she would turn five before the end of the year. Without thought, John and I thought this was a great idea, but in hindsight, Janiya needed more time to mature. Well, Janiya began Kindergarten. Towards the middle of the year, we started receiving complaints from her teachers: "Janiya is not focused; she's very sweet and plays well with the other children, but when it's time to read, she is singing instead of reading." It went from that to "She's not focused and is easily distracted." So, like any mother, I sat Janiya down to have long talks with her. I explained to her that school time is for learning, not only playing. She would look at me with her gorgeous eyes and that beautiful smile and say, "Ok mommy." We were able to get her to do well enough for promotion to the 1st grade. When she got to 1st grade, she was a little more mature but still not as mature as she needed to be. Her first-grade teacher had no tolerance and was not willing to take extra time with the few students in the class who required additional help.

Note: we all learn differently. Some of us are more visual, while others of us are literal, and some of us learn by doing the act and physically participating. Well, our children are no different. They too, all learn differently. One person isn't smarter than the other; it's just the *Beauty* of our differences. When properly channeled, each learning method can complement the other. As Janiya moved further into the year, her first-grade teacher began to attempt to label a few of the kids, Janiya being one of them. One day she sent Janiya home paperwork stating my daughter had a problem with comprehension. The information also said Janiya was unable to grasp the content, and she needed placement in the Special Education program for the rest of her school years, from first to twelfth grade.

I wasn't mortified because of the program. I am grateful some programs are in place to help those students in need. I was mortified because I knew they were misdiagnosing my child out of laziness.

Janiya had no problems with comprehension at home. She could sing the words to every song we played, memorize her favorite books, and understand the rules of any game we played. However, I did notice Janiya was just like her dad in a few areas. One of them being, if she was not interested in the presentation, she wasn't going to pay it any mind. You have approximately five minutes to grab their attention. In fact, if it looks boring, she will check out on you mentally before you get started. Well, you should know by now what I did when I saw these papers. Yup, I took it to Jesus, but this time I took Janiya with me. I sat down with her, and during our reading time, we also read scriptures and prayed together.

We thanked God for helping Janiya with schoolwork, helping her pass tests, and getting good grades. When I left Janiya's room, I went into my room and cried out to God. I put my faith on her making the honor roll and passing all her state tests. Most importantly, I prayed for her mind, for her focus, for her determination, and her confidence. Fast forward to now, Janiya is in the 11th grade and is doing *EXCELLENT*!! She has made the honor roll multiple times! She currently has an 85% average which, we are *Absolutely* ecstatic about. She has passed all her state tests and is now in AP classes, which gives her the advantage of accumulating college credits.

She is creative, talented, and gifted! She just started her own YouTube channel "Janiya's Face," where she shares her gift of creating out of the box makeup looks, and amazing eye shadow combinations that anyone of all ages can wear. She is a self-taught *Makeup Artist* and headed toward one of her dreams to create her own makeup line. She has a few aspirations, but whatever she decides, we know that *GOD'S* plans for her life will be fulfilled.

I shared this story with you because standing on the principles of God with Janiya taught her how to *Bear Fruit*. It taught her to hold on to God's promises, no matter what people say or do. No matter what it looks like during the process at the end of the process, the *Fruit of God's Word* will manifest and come to full fruition in her life. She learned that *God's Word Is True.* I would always tell her if you do your part, *God Will Do His Part.* She is only 16 years old, and she is already learning how to bear fruit. I used to say, "The greatest gift you can give your children is Jesus," and this is true, but now I add on, "*and Principle Living.*" It is one thing to teach them salvation, but teaching them how to live a *Godly Lifestyle* will allow them to become *Fruit Bearers* and experience the *FRUIT of God's Word.* I shared just one of the many examples of bearing fruit with the people in your home. Likewise, by using this same principle outside of my house, I have seen great results in my life. I would go out my way to help people in some way, shape, or form, and then I would walk into places where I needed assistance, and people would automatically walk up to me and help me.

For example, my husband and I had recently purchased a vehicle, and we were extremely grateful and excited. So, on the day of our downtime, we went back to the dealership just to get a few accessories for our new wheels. John and I pulled into the dealership driveway with the plan for me to sit and wait in the car. Immediately this young man comes running outside, walks over to my husband, and asks how he could help. John shares we are there to purchase accessories for our new vehicle. The gentleman says, "Sure, no problem, the accessories are right this way, just let me know what you need." As John looked at all the different accessories, they began to see other items he may want to purchase. So, my husband comes back to the car to get me so I can help him make some wise decisions on our purchase. As soon as we walk back into the dealership, the same young man walks back over to us and says, "I don't know you guys, but I'm going to let you use my discount today. With my discount, everything will be *HALF OFF* the prices you see listed. Please choose whatever you would like to purchase." At this point, I'm look-ing at John thinking, what did you do? He says, "Babe, I only walked in the store!" That day we were able to get more than what we planned and spent less than what we expected. Just as the salesman prom-ised, he gave us 50% off each item. He asked to exchange numbers with John and wanted us to know that we could call him if we needed. Through regular conversations, he has become one of the young men my husband mentors. One day in conversation, the same young man mentioned to John that he never owned a vehicle. He needed a car to get around and, most importantly, back and forth to work. My hus-band pointed him to a good friend of ours that works for a dealership. As God would have it, this young man was able to purchase his first vehicle! I said to John, "Wow, look at God! We are always looking for ways to help others. This young man made a simple gesture to help us, and you were able to connect him to the help he needed." The story doesn't end here! One week later, we received a phone call about a possible business deal. My husband and I think, 'Wow, this is a great idea! We believe that this was a solid deal. We prayed, talked, and had a family meeting with our girls. We decided to go through with the deal. We got on the phone to work out the logistics, and the person we were negotiating with says, "I tell you what, not only can we do this deal with you; we can also include enough money for you to *Pay Off* the vehicle you just purchased." My mouth dropped, I said, "*OMG this is FRUIT*! Not only will we get relief from the car note, but the benefits that we'll receive towards our credit will also be *Great*!" All of this came out of working the principle of *helping* others.

Do you see how working one principle has produced so much fruit? Not only have we benefited from it, but the people involved in this process have also benefited as well. Now because of this testi-mony, *You* are benefiting! The scripture I shared with you earlier explains this perfectly. It says that we should bear fruit, and purposefully use our power, influence, gifts, and talents to do things for others that will be a blessing to them. Reciprocation will be the result, which will create testimonies that you can share with everyone you meet, proving that *God's Principles Work*! The scripture is clear when it says, "So that you would go and bear fruit and keep on bearing, and that your fruit will remain and be lasting, so that whatever you ask of the Father in My name [as My representative] He may give to you."

I have many testimonies I can share with you! The list of fruit from the principles of God I have applied to my life are *Countless*. We have used our home for many years to host our mentoring programs. Our house has become a spiritual, mental, and physical haven for people. We've had young ladies stay with us whom we have nurtured and poured into. We've had whole families stay with us when they had nowhere else to go. I am not telling you this to brag! What I am telling you is that the *Principles of God Work*! People always say to us, your family is beautiful, your girls are role models, and your marriage is an inspiration. They affirm us by saying, "You and John have saved our lives." Our response is always "It's not us; it's *Only God In Us. He Deserves All the Glory*."

The key to seeing fruit in your life is to sincerely, wholeheartedly, with a pure heart want to please God with your life. You adapt your lifestyle to living out the principles of God one by one; no principle is too small. Simply being kind, respectful, helpful, patient, humble, and loving and being generous, pleasant, approachable, encouraging, supportive, consistent, reliable, truthful, honest, and dependable. Moreover, being a person people know they can come to and receive the *Love Of God* is a great place to start. If you can commit, begin using these same principles today, and you will see a tremendous change in your life. You too will begin to *Bear Fruit*, and you will have testimonies to share that will bring out the fruit in others.

I pray this principle resonates with your *Spirit* and encourages you to keep going and commit to principle living. Remember, trees die because they don't bear fruit. So let's not be like those trees. Let's be the *Fruit Bearers* that God created us to *BE*!

FYI, the vehicle that we paid off was my *DREAM VEHICLE*!

"I am the true Vine, and My Father is the vinedresser. Every branch in Me that does not bear fruit, He takes away; and every branch that continues to bear fruit, He [repeatedly] prunes, so that it will bear more fruit [even richer and finer fruit]."
– John 15:1-2 AMP

WALL #4 – LIVING A LIFE OF EXPECTATION

Here we are! We've made it to our last and final wall for this book. I have thoroughly *Enjoyed*, sharing some of my life experiences with you, and most importantly, the principles of God. I feel like we have taken a journey together and have gained revelation, clarity, and insight. Moreover, we were presented with some ways we can make ourselves *Better*. I am *Overwhelmed* with *Gratitude* to have this God-ordained opportunity of sharing with people worldwide through this vehicle of writing. When I was a little girl, I dreamed of being a lot of things, but being an Author was never one of them. Who would've thought this little black girl from the ghetto, a teen mom, with no college degrees would have *Anything* to say that people would want to listen to? Well, I was *Wrong*! I am a witness that *God Exceeds* whatever you can ask or think of! He will also put you in positions you never dreamed of. I am 42 years old, and God is still revealing the gifts and talents I possess and some I didn't know I had! When you avail yourself to Him, you will be *Amazed* at what you can do!

We have discussed so many great principles. I pray every wall in this book will give you the strength, support, structure, and power you need to *Build A Stronger You*. Just like all the other principles, this one is also *vital* to your spiritual, mental, and physical growth. So, let's jump right into it!

Living a Life of Expectation!

When I think about expectation, I can't think of many things in my life where I don't have an expectation. In my mind, even the objects and things we purchase, we buy them because we expect something from them. For instance, if we buy a dining room set, do we not expect the chairs to hold us or the table will stand firm without collapsing? When we go to the mall, do we not expect there will be items ready and available for purchase? When we take medication, do we not expect it to work? When we travel, do we not expect our vehicles, or the train, and or buses to take us to the specific location we have chosen?

So, how can we live life without *Expectation*? Don't get me wrong; it's doable. However, in my opinion, *That Should Never Happen*. Expectation is as necessary to me as the oxygen we need to breathe. Expectation gives me a reason to live! Every day I wake up and say, *I am Expecting something Great to happen to me today*! Every night I go to sleep, I expect to rest well so that I can be energized and prepared for the next day of *Expectation*. This powerful word, *Expectation*, adds to your will to live; it waters and grows the seeds in your life, especially for those of us who are believers and govern our lifestyles by God's principles. If we expect things, then how much more should we expect God? Don't ever let anything or anyone stop your expectation of God! Often, we can allow what we've seen others go through, stories we've heard, or even our life experiences to dull down and deplete our expectations. Remember, we talked about the benefits of salvation earlier in this book? Well, one of the benefits of living a godly lifestyle is through God's Word. He makes promises to us that we can *Expect* to happen in our lives. I know people have disappointed you.

As you already know, people have let me down. However, we will not diminish God by putting Him on the same level as people. Anytime I have been tempted to think that God would disappoint me like people, I remember this scripture.

> "God is not a man, that He should lie, nor a son of man, that He should repent. Has He said, and will He not do it? Or has He spoken, and will He not make it good and fulfill it?"
> — Numbers 23:19 AMP

It is the trick of the devil to crush your *Expectation*. If he can destroy our expectations, he can stop us from hoping, dreaming, desiring, praying, believing, and ultimately having faith in God. Without expectation, we will lose our joy and have no excitement about life. Remember, joy is our strength. I hope you are beginning to see how imperative expectation is. When I think of my life, I see a whole world full of what I am *Expecting God* to do through me and for me! And, I am *Confident He Will* do exactly what He said He would do!

> "Wait for and confidently expect the LORD; Be strong and let your heart take courage; Yes, wait for and confidently expect the LORD."
> — Psalms 27:14 AMP

I remember when one of my mentees said to me, "I don't do better because nobody expects me to do better." My eyes filled with tears, and my heart ached for them as I felt the pain of *Unbelief*. Listen, *Expectation, Faith, and Belief* are relatives. They all roll together, and you can't have one without the other. I started to think, wow, if we as humans are devastated, become stagnant, and feel worthless when people don't expect, believe in, or have faith in us; then how does God feel when we don't *Expect, Believe, or have Faith* in HIM. Of course, He doesn't feel devastated, become stagnant, or feel worthless because He is God. *BUT,* I believe it does hurt His Heart. Yes, God has feelings too. He feels the pain of our *Unbelief,* our *Faithlessness,* and when we don't *EXPECT* Him to fulfill the promises that He has made to us in His word. What I am saying is your Faith pleases God.

> "But without faith, it is impossible to [walk with God and] please Him, for whoever comes [near] to God must [necessarily] believe that God exists and that He rewards those who [earnestly and diligently] seek Him."
> — Hebrews 11:6 AMP

Your *Faith* in, *Belief* in, and *Expectation of God* are necessary ingredients to seeing the promises of God come to fruition in your life. *Expectation is Everything*! We always want a person to do things for us that puts a smile on our faces. Today, I want you to know that living a life of *Expectation* puts a smile on God's face, and it requires Him to move on your behalf according to His word. I've heard some Christians say that God does not *Have* to do anything for you. Well, I disagree. According to the scriptures, when we align our lives with His word, God himself says that He is obligated to fulfill His word.

> "So will My word be which goes out of My mouth; It will not return to Me void (useless, without result), Without accomplishing what I desire, And without succeeding in the matter for which I sent it."
> — Isaiah 55:11 AMP

I love this scripture! It puts a new pep in my step! I received the revelation of this scripture, and it causes me to *EXPECT GOD* in every area of my life. I remember when I was about six months pregnant with my middle daughter Jaelyn. As it is the doctor's standard procedure to test for Down Syndrome, I, too, received this routine test. A few days later, the doctor called my job and told me that the results came back and confirmed that my baby had Down Syndrome. I was hysterical, and I immediately called John and my mom. Well, when they arrived, I remember us going into the back room at my job with some of my coworkers, and we began to pray.

We *Denounced* that report and placed a *DEMAND* on God. According to *His Word*, He is our *HEALER*! Were we tempted to give in to the thoughts of unbelief? Absolutely! However, although tempted, we did not give in! Every time the devil would remind me of what the doctors said, I would remind him of what *GOD SAID*. My doctor wanted me to make a list of other tests and suggested that we see a therapist to prepare ourselves for this disease. Because of my *Expectation,* I instinctively signed a waiver saying I would not be participating in *ANYTHING* associated with that disease. *I EXPECTED GOD* to move on my behalf and to help me deliver a whole and healthy baby with *No Sickness OR Diseases In Her Body*. Well! About four months later, the obstetrician induced my labor. There was a team of doctors in my room waiting for Jaelyn to come out with Down Syndrome as they thought they would have to take special care of her. I pushed her out, and there was a moment of silence that felt like forever. I looked at my doctor as her eyes opened wide like she had seen a ghost. I said to her, "What? What's wrong!" With tears in her eyes, she looked at me and said, *"Nothing, She Is Beautiful!"* As I am sharing this with you, tears of joy still run down my face! Today Jaelyn is 19 years old, and she was recently accepted to attend Fordham University for the Alvin Ailey BFA program. She has *NEVER* had any academic issues and currently has a 3.8 GPA. Yes, she is a beautiful, intelligent, well rounded, determined, creative, and an Anointed Dancer! She is *Very Analytical*, and *Very Strategic*, in her approach to her career and life.

Most importantly, she *LOVES* God, she is a *WORSHIPER*, and as of today, she is still a VIRGIN! Her dream is to become a member of the Alvin Ailey Company and eventually become a dance studio owner so that she can give back to her community. Can I tell you that *GOD HAS EXCEEDED OUR EXPECTATIONS!* So, I want to close out on this remarkable principle. It's very simple, *EXPECT GOD!!*

Expect Him to help you. *Expect Him* to give you the strength, power, and anointing to *Become the Best version of you* than you ever dreamed possible, *And More. Expect Him* to *Always* be by your side. Expect Him to always provide a way of escape from *Everything and Anything* that overwhelms you. Expect Him to *Rescue* you from your troubles. Expect Him to provide for *Your Every Need.* Expect Him to *HEAL* you Physically, Mentally, Emotionally, and Spiritually. Expect you will accomplish all the goals and plans He has for you. Expect to have a positive, life-changing impact on your family, friends, your community, and even total strangers that you meet. Expect to dominate in this life and be a world changer! Expect to be an Awesome, Mother, Father, Sister, Brother, Aunty, Uncle, Cousin, a Role Model that you never dreamed you could be. Expect to attract God's favor! Expect to change atmospheres, conversations, and the way people think, for the better, just by your very presence in a room. Expect to be noticed because God's light shines on you and through you! I can keep going! But let me end here. *EXPECT GOD TO EXCEED ALL OF YOUR EXPECTATIONS!!!*

I have *Expected God* to come through for me in times where I thought I was literally going to lose my mind. *God Has Never Let Me Down!* He has *Always* met and *Exceeded My Expectations*. With Him, you will never *Regret* what you *Expect*.

I pray that I have started and enhanced the fire of *Expectation* in you! Expectation will cause your whole life to change, and I pray that you will never be the same in JESUS NAME.

My dear friends *THANK YOU*, for this opportunity, because of God's amazing grace you can EXPECT, a "Behind These Four Walls TOO." It's not over. It's only the beginning!

"Now to Him who is able to [carry out His purpose and] do superabundantly more than all that we dare ask or think [infinitely beyond our greatest prayers, hopes, or dreams], according to His power that is at work within us, to Him be the glory in the church and in Christ Jesus throughout all generations forever and ever. Amen."
– Ephesians 3:20-21 AMP

CONCLUSION

To those of you reading this book, whether male or female, young or seasoned, married, or single. Wherever you find yourself in life, be encouraged to continue doing your self-work. I have committed my life to creating a better version of *Me* daily. I am enjoying this journey and am amazed at the things that God continues to reveal to *me* concerning *ME*.

I pray this book has added to your life in some way, shape, or form. I pray that you are encouraged to want to invest in a better you. I am a firm believer that what God has for me is for me. I also know that I must be willing to do the work it takes to acknowledge and get rid of my dysfunctions, by divorcing my *"soulish ways,"* renewing my mind, and submitting myself to God. Only then will I be able to receive what He has for me.

Before we end this portion of our journey, I want to ask you to do something for me. Please, promise in times where there is no one to encourage you that you will vow to *Encourage Yourself*. This simple but powerful principle has become part of my daily routine. Just as I commit to bathing, brushing my teeth, and combing my hair daily. I also commit to affirming myself *Daily*.

So, I want to leave you with one of my list of affirmations and encourage you to create affirmations that are tailor-made by you, just for YOU.

AFFIRMATIONS

I thank you God,
that I have a *RELATIONSHIP*
with You!

I was created
in the image of God.

I am fearfully and
wonderfully made.

GOD chose me before
I was in my mother's womb.

I was created to be
a Creative being.

I thank you God that I am
not barren or unfruitful.

I possess everything that
is necessary for life.

I am Disciplined, and I put God first in everything I do.

I thank you, God that you have supplied my needs in Abundance!

I seek Peace in God,
Myself, and Others.

I Hunger and Thirst
after Righteousness.

I am a light in
this dark world.

My presence gives
hope, encourages
forgiveness, and promotes
unconditional love.

I forgive myself and others.

I am healed and whole.

The prosperity on the inside of me makes my success inevitable.

I walk in my purpose because
my eyes are constantly and
consistently on God.

Worry, Anger, Depression, and
Anxiety are only *DISTRACTIONS.*
I will not be *DISTRACTED*.

I am focused, and I hear
God's voice clearly.

Favor goes before me
and prepares my way.

Goodness and mercy follow me,
and through salvation, the blood of
Jesus protects me.

Principle living makes me
Unstoppable

I am committed
to Self-Work.

I position myself
to learn and grow.

I am a giver.

I am excited about life!

I Expect Increase!

I walk in Greatness!

I will have a positive impact on my family, friends, and those I come in contact with daily.

TODAY WILL BE AN
AWESOME DAY IN
JESUS NAME!

Until we meet again!

BLESSINGS!

Love EB